The Seven Seals

of the

Holy Spirit

Books by John Fergusson

Authority
Holy Fire
Heal the Sick
Flies in a Window
Who's in Charge Around Here?
School of Healing Manual
So What?
So What Happened?
So What Next?

The Seven Seals
of the
Holy Spirit

~ God's mandate for revival ~

John Fergusson

© John Fergusson

First published in 2019 by JF Ministries

John Fergusson asserts the moral right
to be identified as the author of this work.

No part of this publication may be reproduced or transmitted in any form or by any means, for the purposes of sale, profit or gain, without permission in writing from the publisher. Otherwise this work may be copied if it is to be distributed free of charge, provided that the text is not altered and the original authorship is acknowledged.

Unless otherwise stated, Biblical quotations are from
The New International Version © 1973, 1978, 1984
by the International Bible Society.

PHILLIPS refers to the New Testament in Modern English, © 1958, 1959, 1960 J.B. Phillips and 1947, 1952, 1955, 1957 The Macmillian Company, New York. Used by permission. All rights reserved.

KJV refers to King James Version, crown copyright.

MSG refers to The Message, © 2002 Eugene H. Peterson,
all rights reserved.
Underline emphases in scripture by author

Published in USA by JF Ministries www.jfm.org.nz

Cover Design by Blue Sky Creative

ISBN: 978-1689054225

5.5 x 8.5 kdp edition

Endorsements

This is not just a nice little collection of good ideas for better church government and personal character management.

This has enough supernatural weaponry to softly scare our sweet but complacent body of believers back into Biblical normality—sorely needed in these trying times.

The work of C.S. Lewis, G.K. Chesterton and D. Martyn Lloyd-Jones I knew and loved; now JF must also be added to any required reading list.

Thank you, John. You have spent a significant portion of your life and heart on this.

—Winkie Pratney, Author and Revivalist

A theology of the Holy Spirit the modern church desperately needs, if we are to complete the mission of making Jesus known to all nations. In this book John gifts us a practical handbook on how we can cooperate with the Holy Spirit in every facet of our lives.

Highly recommended to all and especially church leaders who can use it to teach their people.

—David Peters, Director, Spiritlife Ministries, NZ

John Fergusson is like Indiana Jones to the modern church. His book emanates from his adventures as a man of faith.

When many churches are retreating to safer harbours like pragmatism and reason, Fergusson persuades us to read the New Testament literally as a guide for today's church, embracing the

Holy Spirit as critical in establishing the kingdom of God on earth today.

The Seven Seals of the Holy Spirit reads like an adventure novel through scripture with an invitation to embark on our own faith adventure, setting scripture as the foundation to all we do!

John's view may not represent that of many churches God is using today, but I do believe this book will challenge us to keep the Spirit and his gifts central to all we do.

—Paul de Jong, Senior Pastor, LIFE, New Zealand

Acknowledgements

My thanks first to the Lord Jesus for the inspiration of his Spirit, and the time to write.

Next to my beautiful wife, Bron, who suffers my long hours at the keyboard with great patience, and who proof reads everything.

Thank you brother Robert for clarification of the story about Brian Houston.

Special thanks to John Bevere for his influence on my life and teaching, and for permission to use his material.

Thanks to Rodney, Winkey, David and Paul, whose friendship and guidance I appreciate greatly.

Finally, I want to thank the multitude of Christian leaders around the world for whom "ordinary church" won't do; who are passionate to grow in their faith and *chutzpah*; and who are intent upon flowing in the gifts of the Holy Spirit. You hold the keys to revival.

Contents

Foreword...11

Introduction...13

Chapter 1. The Ministry of the Spirit....................15

Chapter 2. The Nature of the Spirit......................27

Chapter 3. The Promise of the Father..................33

Chapter 4. The Purpose of Seals...........................49

Chapter 5. The Seals – Part 1................................59

Chapter 6. The Seals – Part 2................................81

Chapter 7. The Seal of Authority..........................99

Chapter 8. Should we use Tongues in Church?....109

Chapter 9. Be Eager to Prophesy........................127

Chapter 10. How the Spirit Flows.......................147

Chapter 11. How the Spirit Stops........................161

Chapter 12. Making Godly Decisions..................173

Recommended Reading..183

About the Author..185

Foreword

I have had the privilege of knowing and ministering with John at different times for a number of years, since he came to New Zealand.

I have admired his ministry and been blessed to see some of the fruits of his ministry with numbers being healed and set free through the Holy Spirit's outworking through him. Like John, we give all the credit and glory to God for the indwelling Holy Spirit who has enabled us to accomplish things for God that could be accomplished no other way.

I encourage all who read this book to make very sure you know what it is to be filled with the Holy Spirit, speaking in other tongues, and available to him so you can be more effective than ever before.

If you are not sure of the benefits of being filled with the Holy Spirit, just consider the disciples of Jesus before the day of Pentecost. After they were filled with power from on high (Acts 1:8 & Acts 2:1-4), they were transformed in a mighty way to win thousands to Jesus Christ through mighty signs, wonders and miracles.

God is no respecter of persons; he is looking for ordinary people like you and me today who are filled with the Holy Spirit and are available for him to use and work through.

God bless you.

—Rodney W. Francis (Founder/Director, The Gospel Faith Messenger Ministry. www.gospel.org.nz

Introduction

"What's in the box?" The Mumbai airport customs official tapped the large, silver flight case in my luggage.

"A video projector." My 1990's model weighed twenty kilograms. "It's a gift for a friend." Having served its purpose for us, it was intended to bless a South Indian church.

The officer pursed his lips. "Come with me."

I followed his uniform into the airport's intestines. Behind steel-mesh walls, acres of confiscations lurked, stacked beyond visibility—Aladdin's cave without the lamp.

In a dingy office, he opened a ledger that covered his whole desk, and began to write, very slowly.

After I supplied endless details, he added, "The duty will be two thousand dollars."

"What? It only cost half that, new!"

"If you cannot pay, we impound it," he nodded to the stacks, "and you collect when you depart."

I shrugged in helpless agreement. He wrapped the box in a cobweb of jute string, melted a large glob of sealing wax onto the knots, and stamped. Its unique aroma filled the office.

And sure enough, when I left India weeks later, Customs returned the box intact, the seal untouched.

The experience caused me to begin noticing seals in scripture. And the more I looked, the more I noticed a pattern. For seals keep appearing, for many reasons. *Now it is God who makes both us and you stand firm in Christ. He anointed us, set his seal of ownership on us, and put his Spirit in our hearts as a deposit, guaranteeing what is to come* (2 Corinthians 1:21-22).

What did this mean? What is his seal of ownership? And why is the Spirit a deposit? I determined to find out. The Lord showed me things I've never heard taught or preached; things too important to ignore; things vital to our understanding of our relationship with God, our purpose on earth, and how he enables us to fulfil them.

For the Lord sent the Holy Spirit for very much more than Pentecost, more even than his fruits and his gifts. Scripture is stuffed with insight about his power, his purpose and his presence.

The theme of seals keeps reappearing, like a trademark, unfamiliar until we stop and ask, "Why is that there?" So much of scripture is like that—no other literature yields so much from such applied curiosity. Perhaps it's why he made us curious in the first place.

I don't pretend to be an expert, but each of us has a piece of the patchwork of the revelation of the kingdom of God, and it is our duty and privilege to share it. Some of this I have known for years. Some I have learned recently. But as you read, *test everything. Hold on to the good* (1 Thessalonians 5:21), forget what's not.

I pray this book may add a thread to the eternal tapestry that is the kingdom. And may it inspire you to greater faith, greater service and greater fruitfulness.

Chapter 1

The Ministry of the Spirit

I am tired of boring church meetings!

A few songs (some fast, some slow), the notices, the offering (with or without music), communion (sometimes), the sermon, a closing song, a benediction, tea and coffee. For variety, shuffle the deck.

I've witnessed this from mega-churches in big cities to remote house-groups in the mountains of India. It's what we do. We go through the motions because it's what's expected of us, it's what we were taught, it's what people want, or we simply don't know what else to do.

But reading 1 Corinthians 14, or John 13, or Malachi 1, is this what the Lord intended? For many things we're exhorted to do in our meetings, we never do. I mean, when was the last time you washed someone's feet in church? Jesus washed the disciples feet, and said, *"Now that I, your Lord and Teacher, have washed your feet, you also should wash one another's feet"* (John 13:14). So why don't we?

And when was the last time you saw this in church? *And if a revelation comes to someone who is sitting down, the first speaker should stop* (1 Corinthians 14:30). Can you imagine? Or this: *When you come together, everyone has a hymn, or a word of instruction, a revelation, a tongue or an interpretation* (1 Corinthians 14:26).

I want to see the kingdom.

The church I see doesn't have walls. It is not consumed with buildings and structures, instruments and equipment, programmes and strategies, appointments and committees. (Lord, save us from committees.)

This is the church I see:
A community of people filled with the Holy Spirit; full of enthusiasm, power and grace; taking the gospel of the kingdom and the power of God to the villages, cities, and nations, unashamed and unafraid. Healing the sick, casting out demons, raising the dead, then coming together to share supernatural testimonies, to encourage each other, to prophesy the word of the Lord, and to train new believers to disciple others.

This community is filled with life, with love, with power, with resources, with courage, with vision, with fruitfulness. It cares not for discomfort, for hindrances, for setbacks, for lack, for rejection, for stumbling blocks, but presses on with passion to fulfil the Great Commission before the Lord returns.

This is the church I see. This is the church that ministers in the power of the Spirit. It knows about the seven seals.

~ ✝ ~

"Will you preach in our slum?" David asked.

"Of course," my mouth said. My head wasn't so sure.

He wove his old motorbike through the back streets of Pune, India, and stopped by a dirt alley. "We have to walk from here."

We negotiated putrid puddles between rows of hovels, and came to a building site—concrete pillars and floors, but without walls. Upstairs, insects swarmed round a single light bulb, beneath which a crowd had gathered. Two played guitars, one with only four strings, the other in a different key. Neither could sing. But the worshippers lifted their saris and danced, their faces alight with inexpressible joy, for a whole hour.

When my turn came, I said, "I cannot teach you anything. You know the Lord better than I."

That's church.

More recently, after a school of healing in Nepal, we sent two of our team to a neighbouring village to minister to a paralysed lady. On the way, they met another lady, dizzy and in pain. They laid hands on her and she was immediately healed.

When they arrived at the village, the paralysed lady pointed to her eyes. She was partially blind as well. After some minutes of ministry, the Lord healed her eyes. Our team continued with her until she got up and walked across the house. She'd been in bed for five years. Her husband, an unbeliever, was deaf. They ministered to him too, and he received his hearing. Then they led him to Christ.

A few days later we were teaching healing near the Beldangi Refugee Camp in Eastern Nepal. A doctor had told a young mother her right eye would never see again. After the first session, she was seeing clearly in that eye. As she gave her testimony an old man at the back spontaneously received his sight.

That's church.

In 1996, I had the privilege of attending Jackie Pullinger's church in Hong Kong. Worship was intense and uplifting, after which the congregation began to move in gifts of the Spirit. One brought a tongue, another interpreted. Then another. Back and forth they came, thick and fast. Prophecies, tongues, words of encouragement, as the Spirit flowed. Many of the four hundred present were in tears.

That's church.

Standing on a shipping container in Lagos, Nigeria, in

November, 2000, I gazed out at 1.6 million people. The crowd stretched over seventy acres, almost as far as the eye could see. On the right side, people streamed into the ground, filling a four-lane highway, a human river a hundred metres wide. There were five such entrances.

The night before, Reinhard Bonnke had called for the Spirit to fall. As the crowd lifted their voices in new tongues, a roar ascended to heaven like the voice of the Lord himself—*Then I heard what sounded like a great multitude, like the roar of rushing waters and like loud peals of thunder, shouting: "Hallelujah! For our Lord God Almighty reigns"* (Revelation 19:6).

The roar had the hiss of heavy rain, the thunder of waterfalls, the ebb and flow of surf, the rush of rapids. Across the crowd the sound washed like waves of the sea, a heavenly Mexican wave, too fast to be designed by man.

That's church.

As I crested the wall of Old Jerusalem, an elderly Israeli approached me, proffering a begging cup.

I smiled at him. "What is it you want?"

He replied in English. "What I would really like is a good coffee."

We repaired to a local cafe.

"Are you a tourist?" he asked.

I explained I was researching a book about Jesus. "Do you know him?"

He shook his head. I shared the gospel with him.

"Would you like to give your life to the Lord?"

He nodded, and I led him in a prayer of salvation.

That's church.

Ministering in the Spirit

Every disciple of Jesus is a child of God, and every child of God, a priest. *But you are a chosen people, a royal <u>priesthood</u>, a holy nation, a people belonging to God, that you may declare the praises of him who called you out of darkness into his wonderful light* (1 Peter 2:9).

Therefore every Christian believer is a minister of the gospel, whether or not we are gifted with the office of apostle, prophet, evangelist, pastor, teacher, or any other form of service. (As a teacher, I note my place in the list!)

Ministry is giving. When Peter and John healed the crippled beggar in Acts 3:6, Peter said to him, *"Silver or gold I do not have, but what I have I give you."* In order to perform any ministry of the kingdom, we must know we have something—and give it away.

What do we have?

Paul describes it at length in 2 Corinthians chapters 3 and 4. Why not read them now or have your Bible handy? *Therefore, since through God's mercy we have <u>this ministry</u>, we do not lose heart* (2 Corinthians 4:1). What ministry? Go back a few verses.

Now if the ministry that brought death, which was engraved in letters on stone, came with glory, so that the Israelites could not look steadily at the face of Moses because of its glory, fading though it was, will not the <u>ministry of the Spirit</u> be even more glorious? (2 Corinthians 3:7-8).

First, Paul contrasts the fading glory of the Old Covenant with the "surpassing glory" of the New. The Old brought death, the New, life; the Old, darkness, the New, light; the Old, bondage, the New, freedom, the Old, glory, the New, ever-increasing glory! This is the ministry of the Spirit.

Glory

Second Corinthians 3:18 says *we are being transformed into his likeness with ever-increasing glory.* But doesn't everyone know the Lord doesn't share his glory? Doesn't he say in Isaiah 48:11, *"I will not yield my glory to another?"*

Yes, he does. However, in the Isaiah passage the Lord is actually rebuking Israel for ascribing his works to their idols. Look at verse 5: *"Therefore I told you these things long ago... so that you could not say, 'My idols did them.'"*

And in the often-quoted, parallel scripture, *"I am the LORD; that is my name! I will not give my glory to another or my praise to idols"* (Isaiah 42:8), it's again clear the issue is idolatry.

This was the sin of the Pharisees that made Jesus so angry—ascribing the work of the Holy Spirit to the devil and his demons. He'd just driven out a demon, and the mute man spoke. *But some of them said, "By Beelzebub, the prince of demons, he is driving out demons"* (Luke 11:15).

At his most sarcastic, the Lord replied, *"But if I drive out demons by the finger of God, then the kingdom of God has come to you"* (Luke 11:20). Why did he use the strange phrase, *finger of God*? When Jesus uses odd language, it's time to check out the Old Testament.

Moses and Aaron performed the first two plagues of blood and frogs in Egypt. Pharaoh's magicians copied them. But they were unable to copy the third plague of gnats with their magic arts. Then *the magicians said to Pharaoh, "This is the finger of God." But Pharaoh's heart was hard and he would not listen, just as the LORD had said* (Exodus 8:19).

The Pharisees knew the story by heart. Jesus was really saying to them, "Pharaoh's magicians recognised the Holy Spirit at work, but you people don't, because your hearts are as hard as Pharaoh's." Ouch!

In fact, Jesus <u>wants</u> to share his glory, not with idols, but with us. Not only in eternity (*For our light and momentary troubles are achieving for us an eternal glory that far outweighs them all,* 2 Corinthians 4:17), but also now. Here is 2 Corinthians 3:18 in full: *And we, who with unveiled faces all reflect the Lord's glory, are being transformed into his likeness with ever-increasing glory, which comes from the Lord, who is the Spirit.* It's already happening.

This glory comes from the Lord through his divine wisdom, through persecution, and through those we lead to Christ.

In fact, glory is the theme of the Lord's parting prayer in John 17. In the final section, he prays for *"those who will believe in me"* (John 17:20), and continues, *"I have given them* [that is, all believers] *the glory that you gave me, that they may be one as we are one"* (John 17:22).

And notice the purpose—perfect unity. Glory (*kabad* in Hebrew, *doxa* in Greek) isn't just bright lights. It also means weight, implying authority, reputation, honour, influence and dignity. <u>This</u> glory is the Lord's plan for his church, so that we are united, so that people will believe the Father sent Jesus, and that he loves them. *"May they be brought to complete unity to let the world know that you sent me and have loved them even as you have loved me"* (John 17:23b). That's the goal.

Jesus wants a glorious bride, so that many will come to love him. Don't refuse his glory. Embrace it gladly, but with a tablespoon of reverent fear.

Power

Not only do we have ever-increasing glory, but all-surpassing power! *But we have this treasure in jars of clay to show that this all-surpassing power is from God and not from us* (2 Corinthians 4:7).

It took the Lord four words (two in Hebrew) to create light, but three days to raise Jesus from the dead. And yet Romans 8:11 says, *and if the Spirit of him who raised Jesus from the dead is living in you, he who raised Christ from the dead will also give life to your mortal bodies through his Spirit, who lives in you.* Again, it's the Father who gives life <u>through</u> his Spirit—from the one comes the word, from the other, the action. *For it is his mouth that has given the order, and his Spirit will gather them together* (Isaiah 34:16b).

The words Spirit and power appear together over fifty times in scripture. Power is who he is. Therefore power is what, or rather who, we have.

> Faith pushes God's buttons

When Jesus walked on the earth, he just leaked. *The people all tried to touch him, because power was coming from him and healing them all* (Luke 6:19). When the woman with the issue of blood touched him, he felt the power leave.

Faith is the channel through which the power flows. In his home town and in Jerusalem, Jesus did fewer miracles because of their lack of faith. But when people have prayed, when people are expecting, when people are trusting Jesus, the Spirit moves. Sometimes he hovers, but the Lord cannot resist faith. Hebrews 11:6 says, "*Without faith it is impossible to please God.*" The reverse must also be true—<u>with</u> faith, it is impossible <u>not</u> to please him. If God has buttons somewhere about his Person, faith certainly pushes them!

Many believe they only have a tiny drop of the Spirit. Only slightly anointed. But the Holy Spirit is a Person, not a thing. If you invite me to dinner, I don't first send my tongue to check your culinary skills. When my tongue arrives, you get the rest of me too.

When the Spirit is within us, <u>all</u> his power and gifts are available to us. Either we are anointed, or we aren't. Either we have his power, or we don't. And scripture is clear—if we are saved, the Spirit lives in us. We have power.

And, astonishingly, if we have the Holy Spirit's power, we are able to do all that the Holy Spirit can do to extend the kingdom of God. The only limit is our own faith. This is beyond our comprehension. But didn't Jesus say, *"You will do even greater things"*? When faced with the impossible, ask yourself, "Is the Spirit able to do this?" If yes, then let him do it through you.

Do we have to be baptised in the Spirit before we can minister? No, the disciples were healing the sick and casting out demons long before Pentecost. But we do need the baptism, as we will see.

Freedom

Now the Lord is the Spirit, and where the Spirit of the Lord is, there is freedom (2 Corinthians 3:17). This means freedom from sin, guilt, condemnation, oppression, fear, sickness, addictions, spiritual blindness and the Law. It also means freedom for relationship, eternal life, abundant life, power, glory and even freedom! The lists are endless.

But I want to highlight one often-neglected freedom—authority. In my book of that title, I have tried to give a comprehensive, Biblical account. Its importance for the ministry of the Spirit cannot be overstated.

The word for authority in Greek is *exousia*, which literally means the right, permission, or freedom to act. Jesus said, *"All authority in heaven and on earth had been given to me"* (Matthew 28:18).

Now authority is delegated on command, so whenever Jesus commanded his disciples (and therefore us) he was transferring authority. When he says to make disciples, or heal the sick, or love one another, we not only have the freedom to do so, but are expected to do so without needing further permission. The command is enough. Authority is transferred.

And not only are we responsible to fulfil the command, we can trust his endorsement too. Jesus said authority had been given to him. He hadn't taken it for himself—that would be rebellion. All authority begins with the Father and is delegated. Therefore the Father endorses Jesus when he does what the Father asks. In the same way, when Jesus delegates his authority to us, he endorses his command by supporting our actions. *"And surely I am with you always"* (Matthew 28:20) is not merely a promise of his eternal presence, but an endorsement of our obedient ministry. "I am rooting for you," declares our greatest Cheerleader!

So whenever we do what he commanded us to do, the Holy Spirit is right there with us, fulfilling his word. It is just as though Jesus himself was doing it, because he delegated it. Did the demons obey Jesus? Then they must obey us. Did sickness leave? Then it must for us.

Competence

But how can this be? We feel so helpless. Perhaps because we have fixed our eyes on the jars of clay instead of the treasure? On what is seen instead of what is unseen?

Paul addresses these very fears. *Such confidence as this is ours through Christ before God. Not that we are competent in ourselves to claim anything for ourselves, but our competence comes from God* (2 Corinthians 3:4-5.)

Our jars of clay are supremely incompetent. We know that full well. But we don't look to the clay, we look to the King, and he has made us competent. Our ministry is in the Name of Jesus, in the power of the Spirit, with the endorsement of the Father. All heaven is for us; who can be against us? It's not our competence, but his. And if he is able, we are too.

Courage

Therefore we can approach the ministry of the Spirit with confidence. Not only that, but *since we have such a hope, we are very bold* (2 Corinthians 3:12). We may only need a mustard seed of faith, but we often feel we need a bucketful of courage! The exhortations, "Be strong and courageous, do not be afraid, do not fear, do not worry, have courage, do not be terrified, do not be discouraged," echo throughout scripture, because the Lord knows how we feel.

And anyway, this is not our ministry. It's his.

What we give

Last year our church packed twenty thousand Christmas boxes, distributing them through local charities to needy families: The knock on the door. The puzzled face. The explosion of joy. The cries and tears of the children unwrapping gifts they would never have had.

We are merely the postmen of the kingdom of God. The gifts of the Spirit are to give away.

In a church one day, a young man about my height came for healing. He suffered from scoliosis and couldn't sit without pain.

I laid my hand on his back and chatted. "What do you do?"

"Oh, I'm a drummer. But it's very hard to still on the stool for long."

We talked some more, when I realised he was now noticeably taller than me.

> The gifts of the Spirit are to give away

Feeling rather foolish, I said, "Did you just grow?"

"Oh," he said, very matter-of-fact, "the doctors said I would be two inches taller if my back was healed." He felt his back and began shouting, "Far out! Far out!"

He called his friends to feel his back, then pointed to a chair in the auditorium. "That's the most uncomfortable one here." He sat, shaking his head, "Far out." His girlfriend was in tears.

Humanitarian aid and serving, healing and deliverance, preaching and teaching are all wonderful, but the most important gift we have is the gospel. Jesus pointed out, *"If your eye causes you to sin, pluck it out. It is better for you to enter the kingdom of God with one eye than to have two eyes and be thrown into hell"* (Mark 9:47). There is no other message to touch it. No other religions will share it. And everyone has a right to hear it.

I've had the huge privilege of watching more people saved than most Christians. Every time it touches my heart, whether one person, or a million. Yesterday, a friend walking her dog noticed a man sitting in his car in a nearby car park. He was still there when she returned. Prompted by the Spirit, she approached and introduced herself. The Lord gave her words of knowledge about his situation, which proved a huge comfort to him. Then she led him to Christ.

I am convinced our reluctance to minister in the Spirit comes out of a lack of assurance of what we have and how to give it away. As I said, the Holy Spirit is given to us for much more than power. But who exactly is this Spirit—what is he like, and what does he do?

Chapter 2

The Nature of the Spirit

We cannot advance the kingdom of God without the Holy Spirit, and we cannot flow with the Spirit without a glimpse of who he is. It all began with him.

In the beginning God created the heavens and the earth. ²Now the earth was formless and empty, darkness was over the surface of the deep, and the Spirit of God was hovering over the waters (Genesis 1:1-2).

When Moses wrote the first five books of the Bible he didn't have headings and fancy fonts! So verse one is his headline for what we now call the first two chapters.

The Hebrew for God here is *Elohim*. The *–im* makes it plural, but not just plural. It means 'more than two'.

Verse two tells how things were <u>before</u> creation: formless (without structure), empty (without matter), and dark (without energy). What was the Spirit doing? Hovering! The Hebrew root is *rachaph*, meaning brooding, or gently waiting, like a hen on her eggs, waiting for the moment. Hovering is waiting too, but isn't idle. A hovering kestrel is flying, searching for its dinner. A hovering helicopter is active. But nothing is happening yet.

So what was the Spirit waiting for? Verse three: *And God said, "Let there be light," and there was light.* God spoke, and like a runner on the starting blocks, the Spirit went into action. The word "let" suggesting the whole Godhead was straining, even desperate, to begin.

The Spirit waited, longing for God to speak. Nothing has changed. He always does and always will.

The Spirit is Lord

Now the Lord is the Spirit, and where the Spirit of the Lord is, there is freedom (2 Corinthians 3:17). Romans 8:9 and Philippians 1:19 describe him as the Spirit of Jesus.

In Matthew 28:19, *"Therefore go and make disciples of all nations, baptizing them in the name of the Father and of the Son and of the Holy Spirit,"* the word 'name' is singular. One God, three Persons. (Don't you love how our God is beyond description or understanding? Would you want a God you could get your head around? A thousand times, no!)

So the Holy Spirit is the third person of the Trinity, and just as much God as the Father and the Son. If Jesus is our Lord, then the Spirit is our Lord too, equally to be worshiped, and equally to be submitted to.

The Bible tells us the Holy Spirit both speaks and loves, but can also be grieved and blasphemed. You cannot blaspheme a thing. Jesus calls him, "he" six times in one verse: *"But when he, the Spirit of truth, comes, he will guide you into all truth. He will not speak on his own; he will speak only what he hears, and he will tell you what is yet to come"* (John 16:13). So he's not a "which" or a "that", but a "who".

The Spirit is Immanuel

The coming of Jesus was announced by Isaiah. *"The virgin will be with child and will give birth to a son, and they will call him Immanuel"—which means, "God with us"* (Matthew 1:23). While Jesus walked the earth, he was Immanuel.

However, Jesus said, *"Unless I go away, the Counsellor will not come to you; but if I go, I will send him to you"* (John 16:7). In Jesus, the Spirit was constrained into one Person, one place and one time. Now that Jesus sits enthroned beside the Father, the Holy Spirit remains. He is the new Immanuel.

Supernatural

What is supernatural to us is natural to God. He made the whole thing in the first place. The Lord is not a deist, hiding in heaven with his arms folded. Like a potter with a stubborn lump of clay, his earnest fingers penetrate every corner of creation, working his masterpiece with a vision in his heart. Miracles are merely a window into his world.

The kingdom of God <u>is</u> supernatural. We can do nothing in the kingdom without the power of the Spirit. *For the kingdom of God is not a matter of talk but of power* (1 Corinthians 4:20). A powerless church is merely a religious club. We reflect the Lord's glory, or we have nothing to offer the world.

But here is the challenge: Jesus said, *"I tell you the truth, <u>anyone</u> who has faith in me will do what I have been doing. He will do even greater things than these, because I am going to the Father"* (John 14:12). Ridiculous? I used to think so, and that was my problem.

> Jesus said, "Anyone who has faith in me will do what I have been doing"

I couldn't believe this Scripture, being convinced that Jesus performed his miracles (and in the context of John 14 we are talking miracles) because he was the Son of God. And of course he is. So it's no surprise he could walk on water, multiply loaves and fishes and raise the dead. Of course he could. He's God.

However, Jesus also said, *"I tell you the truth, the Son can do nothing by himself"* (John 5:19a). In Philippians 2:7 [Phillips], Paul says *"He stripped himself of all privilege."* While he never surrendered his divinity, he became a man, with no more or less power than a man, though without sin. So if the Son could do nothing because he was the Son, how <u>did</u> he heal and deliver?

Jesus didn't begin his ministry until, coming up out of the River Jordan, he was baptised in the Holy Spirit. He was led by the Spirit into the desert, and *returned to Galilee in the power of the Spirit* (Luke 4:14). A few verses later, he laid out his modus operandi: *"The Spirit of the Lord is on me, because he has anointed me..."* (Luke 4:18a). That's how he could preach the good news, heal the broken-hearted, recover the sight of the blind, and release the oppressed. By the Spirit.

When Jesus walked on the earth, he laid aside his divine power in order to demonstrate how a man or woman, filled with the Holy Spirit, may be enabled to advance the kingdom of God. Therefore John 14:12 is not ridiculous at all. We <u>can</u> do even more than Jesus did, when we too have faith in Jesus and are filled with the same Holy Spirit.

But without the Spirit, we are powerless. We can preach, but save no one. We lay hands, but cannot heal. We command demons, but cannot deliver. We can change a person's soul (his mind, his will, his emotions), but it takes the Spirit to renew a man's spirit.

The word "supernatural" is half "super" and half "natural"! With his passion for relationship, the Lord longs to involve every believer in his work. We <u>cannot</u> "do" the supernatural without him; he <u>will</u> not do it without us. (My book, *Authority*, explains why.)

His "super" part moves beyond the usual order of his creation; our "natural" part is the obedience to risk what we see as impossible, stepping out as though we can, knowing we can't. He simply requires trust. We are creator-designed to be interdependent, both with the Lord, and each other.

"*For nothing is impossible <u>with</u> God*" (Luke 1:37). It's the partnership of our obedience and his power. God's plan for our planet cannot be fulfilled without the Holy Spirit and will not be fulfilled without his servants, the church, because, by his grace, we have this relationship.

His plan hasn't changed. He began with the Spirit, and will continue with him. He is the way God works, and therefore the way the Lord works through the church. The Spirit is, we are about to discover, our secret weapon.

The Spirit moves

The Hebrew word for Spirit is *Ruach*, meaning 'breath'. Breath is active, always moving. So he is wind, not still air; streams of living water, not a stagnant pond. He is flowing oil; fire, not wood—always moving, always changing, always creative, never the same as yesterday. He may move here today, but, like a subterranean fire, he will move on tomorrow. Always present, but always responding to the word of God and faith. Waiting for the Word.

> In the world, we become discouraged. The Spirit lifts our vision to restore our heaven-view

Where, and how, will the Spirit breathe tomorrow? Revivals seem unpredictable, random even. But not to God! *For the eyes of the LORD range throughout the earth to strengthen those whose hearts are fully committed to him* (2 Chronicles 16:9a). The Spirit moves wherever he finds true faith in the Son.

But, embedded in the world, we quickly become discouraged. Our eternal inheritance seems so distant, so unlikely, so potentially ephemeral in our minds, we hunger for reassurance of its truth.

We <u>know</u> it's true, but how can it be? We need a knowledge more concrete, a testimony weightier than tablets of stone in an ancient box. We need a receipt signed by the Lord himself. Actually, we already have it; we are drawing closer to the seals.

Chapter 3

The Promise of the Father

In Soweto, South Africa, inside the largest tent in the world, I watched a young girl's arm grow, from withered to normal, in ten seconds.

It was 1984. I'd been a Christian for five years, but my scientifically-trained mindset needed logical explanations. A balloon. A spare arm. Prestidigitation. (I am embarrassed to confess my thoughts.) Finally, the tears of her mother standing beside her convinced me what I'd witnessed was real. My worldview had to change. Don't we find that so hard?

But these people knew something I didn't, and had something I hadn't. Meanwhile, others around me were praising the Lord loudly, in tongues. I knew of this manifestation of course, but had considered it, well... unscientific. Perhaps there was something in it after all? Leaving my friends, I moved to the far side of the tent, and tried speaking in the Spirit. Nothing. I tried singing, and new words came. I sang louder. More words.

"You're just making it up. That's baby language."

I knew enough by then to know the devil when I heard him. "Okay, so I'll just go faster," and for a wonderful half an hour I worshiped the Lord, singing and shouting, with thirty thousand others, in a new heavenly language.

"What happened to you?" my friends said, when I rejoined them.

I beamed.

"You've been baptised in the Holy Spirit!"

I beamed some more.

The experience changed my life, (it's meant to). However, I would not recommend my very delayed pathway, as I believe God has a better plan.

God's Strategy

Jesus said, *"I will build my church, and the gates of Hades will not overcome it"* (Matthew 16:18). His <u>purpose</u> is to establish his kingdom on earth as it is in heaven, through the church.

His <u>method</u> is, and always has been, through the Holy Spirit: *"Not by might, nor by power, but by my Spirit," says the LORD Almighty* (Zechariah 4:6). And again, *"And afterward, I will pour out my Spirit on all people. Your sons and daughters will prophesy, your old men will dream dreams, your young men will see visions"* (Joel 2:28). How does this work in practice?

Moses was overwhelmed by the task of administering several million people. His wise father-in-law, Jethro, advised delegation. But *the LORD said to Moses: "Bring me seventy of Israel's elders... and I will take of the Spirit that is on you and put the Spirit on them. They will help you carry the burden of the people so that you will not have to carry it alone"* (Numbers 11:16-17). Delegation was fine, but it wasn't enough. The Lord wanted them to operate in the power of the Spirit.

They weren't preaching or healing. They were merely to judge "the simple cases" of the people's problems. And when the Spirit fell on them, they began prophesying! That might seem overkill for a simple administration job, but the Lord knows what is needed.

When the twelve apostles faced a similar situation in Acts 6, they picked seven to serve dinner. But their qualifications? *Known to be full of the Spirit and wisdom* (Acts 6:3b). Of course anyone can serve dinner, with or without the Spirit. But with the Spirit more happens than just food.

In the book of Judges, the Israelites regularly needed deliverance. Then the Spirit of the Lord came in power on Othniel, Gideon, Jephthah and Samson. The Lord stripped Gideon's army to a miniscule troop of three hundred, yet he was able to vanquish the Midianite army, *thick as locusts,* whose *camels could no more be counted than the sand on the seashore* (Judges 7:12). The Lord was fulfilling Leviticus 26:8, *a hundred of you will chase ten thousand,* precisely to point out that it couldn't be man. It had to be the Spirit of God.

Despite standing a head taller than anyone else, Saul son of Kish was naturally shy. When Samuel anointed him king, I imagine the young man was overwhelmed. On his way home, Saul met a procession of prophets. Then *the Spirit of God came upon him in power, and he joined in their prophesying* (1 Samuel 10:10).

In these Old Testament stories, the Spirit came upon the Lord's anointed in power, or gave wisdom or encouragement for particular situations. All that was about to change.

Our purpose

First of all, why are we saved? Yes, we are saved <u>from</u> eternal destruction. Thank God! We are saved <u>for</u> an abundant life now. What grace! We are saved <u>to be</u> the bride of Christ. That's too wonderful to understand. But there's more.

One key is buried in Galatians 3:14, but we'll have to dig. *He redeemed us in order that the blessing given to Abraham might come to the Gentiles* [Greek: ethne] *through Christ Jesus, so that by faith we might receive the promise of the Spirit.* 'Ethne' means non-Jewish nations or Gentiles, which is most of us.

This verse contains a succession of consequences—"in order

that" and "so that". Taking the second first, <u>how</u> do we receive the blessing?

Paul spoke about that a few verses earlier (verses 8-9): *The Scripture foresaw that God would justify the Gentiles* [ethne] <u>*by faith,*</u> *and announced the gospel in advance to Abraham: "All nations* [ethne] *will be blessed through you." So* <u>*those who have faith*</u> *are blessed along with Abraham, the man of faith* (Galatians 3:6-9).

All nations, meaning you and me, may access the same blessing given to Abraham, by faith in the gospel of Jesus Christ. So we qualify if we believe.

Secondly, <u>why</u> are we redeemed? To receive Abraham's blessing! And what is that? Galatians 3:6 tell us: *Consider Abraham: "He believed God, and it was credited to him as righteousness."*

Abraham's blessing was righteousness. God gifted Abraham righteousness because he believed God would keep his promises. This is <u>the</u> foundational doctrine of our faith; we are gifted Jesus' righteousness by believing that he, the Son of God, died in our place and rose again from the dead. It is a gift received by faith. Do you believe? Then you too have the same gift of righteousness. His righteousness, not yours. It cannot be earned; you cannot earn a gift.

Righteousness is a legal concept, meaning right-standing before God. In a court of law, with the Lord as judge, you will be declared innocent. When you believe, your name is written in the Lamb's book of life, and at the great white throne judgement in the book of Revelation, you go free. Righteousness is not the same as purity, sanctification, or holiness, although it leads to those things, but is a stamp of approval, as we will discover.

So now we can paraphrase the first half of Galatians 3:14 a little further: We are redeemed so that we might be given the gift of righteousness. The graphic parallel is of a wealthy businessman purchasing a slave in a market, putting his own mark on the slave's forehead, and then setting him free.

And now the second consequence: We are given this gift of righteousness *so that by faith we might receive the promise of the Spirit.* We cannot receive the promise of the Spirit until we have received the gift of righteousness. Why not? Because he's a <u>Holy</u> Spirit! It's one of the reasons for the seven seals, and therefore this book.

> We are redeemed to receive the gift of righteousness

Having received the gift of righteousness, we are then free to receive, also by faith, *the promise of the Spirit.* What did Paul mean by this phrase?

The promise

Jesus makes it clear. He told the disciples to *"wait for the gift my Father promised, which you have heard me speak about. For John baptized with water, but in a few days you will be baptized with the Holy Spirit"* (Acts 1:4-5). So the promise of the Father is the baptism with the Holy Spirit.

He'd already spoken about this. Just before he died, Jesus said, *"And I will ask the Father, and he will give you another Counsellor to be with you forever—the Spirit of truth"* (John 14:16-17a). And ten verses later he added, *"But the Counsellor, the Holy Spirit, whom the Father will send in my name* [that's the promise], *will teach you all things and will remind you of everything I have said to you."* The coming of the Spirit is the gift of the Father.

Jesus also said when the Spirit comes you will know! It would be an experience, not just a revelation or a new understanding of God. The disciples saw flames, heard wind, and spoke in languages they'd never learned. It was such a dramatic event it attracted both a crowd and immediate persecution.

To be baptised is to be immersed. *Baptizo* is a Greek word from the dyeing industry that we've adopted, having no suitable translation. When the cloth enters the vat, the dye colours the cloth—the cloth in the dye, the dye in the cloth.

Summarising Galatians 3:14 again, we have been redeemed in order to be made righteous, in order to be baptised with the Holy Spirit. Therefore the baptism with the Holy Spirit is not just an added extra for a few keen believers, but an integral part of the purpose of our salvation. It's not even a badge of Pentecostal denominations. It is one of the main reasons we're saved!

> We've been saved in order to be baptised in the Holy Spirit

It's forever

When Jesus was baptised, he came up out of the water and the Holy Spirit fell on him in the form of a dove. John the Baptist declared, *"I would not have known him, except that the one who sent me to baptize with water told me, 'The man on whom you see the Spirit come down <u>and remain</u> is he who will baptize with the Holy Spirit'"* (John 1:33).

The Holy Spirit had come upon many before, but the "and remain" was new.

Isaiah had prophesied this. *"As for me, this is my covenant with them," says the LORD. "My Spirit, who is on you, and my words that I have put in your mouth will not depart from your mouth, or from the mouths of your children, or from the mouths of their descendants <u>from this time on and forever</u>,"* says the LORD (Isaiah 59:21).

But the "forever" promise hadn't happened until Jesus arose from the Jordan. Does "forever" include us, the church?

Absolutely, yes! We are children of God. We are his descendants and heirs. We inherit Christ's blessings.

The baptism with the Holy Spirit was new. John the Baptist tells us that the one who baptises with the Holy Spirit is the Messiah. It is his unique sign.

And not only is the baptism with the Holy Spirit Jesus' personal sign, he passes it on—he *"will baptise with the Holy Spirit"*! Jesus himself said, *"For John baptized with water, but in a few days you will be baptized with the Holy Spirit"* (Acts 1:5). Nowhere do we read that it's unnecessary, or restricted to a limited time period.

Apollos knew only the baptism of John, that is, of repentance. When he began teaching in Ephesus, Priscilla and Aquila took him to one side and *explained to him the way of God more adequately* (Acts 18:26). Evidently he didn't know about the baptism with the Spirit, because in the following passage Paul comes across some disciples whom Apollos has evidently taught. They'd never heard of the Spirit. When taught "more adequately" by Paul, they too were baptised with the Holy Spirit.

There are still many believers, indeed many denominations, who either dismiss the baptism with the Holy Spirit as unnecessary or even not from God. But it's a gift from the Lord Jesus himself, intended for every Christian believer. It's how we know we belong to him. Wouldn't you want all he has to offer?

A warning

Before we look at Pentecost, a note of caution. If the baptism with the Holy Spirit is forever, it would be easy to become complacent. After all, now I am filled, now I can speak in tongues, why should I struggle and fight? I've arrived haven't I? All I need do is wait for my homecoming and spend eternity with Jesus.

At the end of 1 Corinthians 9, Paul describes how disciplined he needs to be. Read this carefully: *No, I beat my body and make it my slave so that after I have preached to others, I myself will not be disqualified for the prize. For I do not want you to be ignorant of the fact, brothers, that our forefathers were all under the cloud and that they all passed through the sea. They were all baptized into Moses in the cloud and in the sea. They all ate the same spiritual food and drank the same spiritual drink; for they drank from the spiritual rock that accompanied them, and that rock was Christ. Nevertheless, God was not pleased with most of them; their bodies were scattered over the desert* (1 Corinthians 9:27-10:5).

I've deliberately joined this passage across the chapter break, since we often miss the implications. Chapter 10 begins with the word "for" (underlined). When you find a "for", ask what it's for!

This passage is a warning against falling away through complacency. All but two of the Israelites died in the desert because of their idolatry, immorality and grumbling. Yet they had all drunk from the rock that was Christ. They had all been "baptised into Moses". What does that mean?

Passing through the waters of the Dead Sea symbolises being baptised in water. They were "saved" in the sense they'd escaped from Egypt, and found the Rock.

The cloud refers to the pillar of cloud that led them during the day, and became a pillar of fire by night. It guided and protected them throughout their journey. We know the Holy Spirit is our Guide, so the cloud represents the Spirit.

Therefore Paul is saying the Israelites were "saved", they were baptised symbolically, both in water and the Holy Spirit, and yet perished before reaching the Lord's purpose for them—the Promised Land.

We dare not be complacent, but should be willing to beat our bodies, that is, be disciplined like Paul. We aren't called to rest on our laurels, enjoying the journey, and ignoring the plight of those around us. The baptism with the Holy Spirit is a magnificent gift given to us because millions need Jesus, and there's work to do.

The lower room

What actually happened at Pentecost? It's always been taught the disciples were in the Upper Room when the Spirit fell. Actually the scripture doesn't say that! Acts 2:2 says they were sitting in a house, so why the confusion? And does it matter? I believe it does.

After Jesus ascended to heaven on the Mount of Olives, the eleven remaining apostles returned to Jerusalem. *When they arrived, they went upstairs to the room where they were staying* (Acts 1:13a). This is where we get the upper room idea. So this was the men's dormitory.

However, in the next verse, we read, *they all joined together constantly in prayer, along with the women and Mary the mother of Jesus, and with his brothers.* Now the women would certainly not have been sharing digs with the men! Therefore this refers to separate prayer meetings and would <u>not</u> have been held in the upper room, but elsewhere.

In the next verse (Acts 1:15) we read that Peter chaired the committee meeting of Acts 1 with a hundred and twenty believers present. Too many for the dormitory.

Then in Acts 2:1, when the Spirit came, *they were all together in one place*, but it cannot have been the upper room because the women were present (it says 'all'), and there were too many of them. So where were they?

A large crowd heard the sound and gathered in curiosity. Then Peter and the Eleven stood up and addressed them. This could only have been at ground level and outside, possibly in a courtyard, which were common in larger houses. So sorry, no upper room!

I hear you saying, "John, who cares?"

The baptism with the Spirit was never intended to be a secret, given to a select few, tucked away in a men's dormitory. Many years ago, Pentecostal believers would hold "tarrying meetings", when they would close the doors of the church from outsiders and "tarry" for the Spirit to fall.

Evangelist Reinhard Bonnke grew up in that tradition. Many years later he held a crusade in the national stadium in Gaborone, Botswana, and the Lord spoke to him to release the Spirit. He was shocked. But when he faithfully obeyed, the Spirit swept across the stadium like a flood, and thousands received the baptism with the Holy Spirit, speaking in tongues.

Preaching to thousands on that first day of Pentecost, Peter declared, *"The promise is for you and your children and for all who are far off—for all whom the Lord our God will call"* (Acts 2:39).

You were redeemed, Galatians 3:14 says, in order to be filled with the Holy Spirit. Pentecost couldn't have happened among unbelievers, because we must first be made righteous by faith in the cleansing power of the blood of Jesus.

> The baptism with the Holy Spirit was never intended to be a secret, given to a select few

Peter explains this divine order by quoting Joel in his astonishing speech. *"I will show wonders in the heaven above and signs on the earth below, blood and fire and billows of smoke"* (Acts 2:19). First, the blood of Jesus, which imputes to us his righteousness; then the fire, a symbol of the Holy Spirit and just seen in tongues on each head; then the smoke, which refers to his glory. And the verse that follows Isaiah 59:21 quoted above?

"Arise, shine, for your light has come, and the glory of the LORD

rises upon you" (Isaiah 60:1). Arise and receive his salvation, shine with the fire of his Spirit, and the glory of the Lord will be made manifest through you. Hallelujah!

Power for all

Jesus said, *"But you will receive power when the Holy Spirit comes on you; and you will be my witnesses in Jerusalem, and in all Judea and Samaria, and to the ends of the earth"* (Acts 1:8).

Later in that chapter, Peter and the apostles hold a meeting to make up the twelve, after Judas killed himself. Peter quotes two scriptures that contradict each other, and they cast lots, which fell to Matthias. We never hear of him again, and we never again read of drawing lots to determine the will of God. Peter's committee meeting added one to the team.

Pentecost moves the church into a new dimension of power. Without preparation or sermon notes, Peter preaches like he's never preached in his life. He quotes heaps of appropriate scriptures, rich with meaning and insight, and three thousand are added in a single day. Man's effort, one. The Spirit's, three thousand plus!

It could be argued that since Jewish tradition usually counted just the men, the actual number was far greater, since the next mention of church growth (Acts 4:4) says, *the number of men grew to about 5,000.*

Several years later, the Apostle Paul finds himself in Athens. Waiting for Silas and Timothy to arrive, he tours the city. He *reasoned* (not preached) in the synagogue and marketplace with those who happened to be there (Acts 17:17). This led to an invitation to speak at their debating chamber, the Areopagus, where Paul delivered a perfectly-structured homily using his considerable oratorical skill, even quoting their own poets. And then we read, *a few men became followers of Paul and believed* (Acts 17:34a).

A <u>few</u> became *followers of Paul*. Not followers of Christ. We don't read of any church planted. Instead, Paul gives up waiting for his friends and hustles to Corinth. What did he pray about on the way? We have a clue.

When I came to you, brothers, I did not come with eloquence or superior wisdom as I proclaimed to you the testimony about God. For I resolved to know nothing while I was with you except Jesus Christ and him crucified. I came to you in weakness and fear, and with much trembling. My message and my preaching were not with wise and persuasive words, but with a demonstration of the Spirit's power, so that your faith might not rest on men's wisdom, but on God's power. (1 Corinthians 2:1-5).

This is astonishing. The great Apostle Paul arrived in Corinth with his tail between his legs, and a dramatic change of tactics. From now on he would stop trying to be erudite and simply <u>demonstrate</u> the power of the Spirit. Wow.

If it was okay for Paul, it's okay for us. So we usually begin this way in our own schools of healing. I call those with a particular problem—painful backs or shoulders, perhaps. Many times a line of sufferers comes forward. We lay hands on them and trust God, according to Mark 16:18, *"they will place their hands on sick people and they will get well."* Almost always the Lord heals some immediately, without any words from us at all.

After a few moments we ask how they feel. If the pain has left, we ask those healed to sit, while we minister again to those standing. We rarely have to repeat this exercise more than three times before everyone is healed, although sometimes, for example if the pain is caused by an evil spirit, we need to command the spirit to leave. We've done this with deaf people, those with bad eyes or other sicknesses, with similar results. God is faithful when we trust him, and put ourselves in a place where we need him.

Jesus said the baptism with the Holy Spirit gives us power to be witnesses. That doesn't just mean sharing the gospel. Healing and deliverance are the greatest witnesses I know to his power and love. When people witness genuine healing and miracles, they find it hard to argue.

It convinced me.

The Lord's perfect timing

First, some math. Acts 1:3 says Jesus appeared to his disciples for forty days after his resurrection. Adding the days in the tomb, we know he ascended forty-two days after Passover, the day he died. Pentecost means fiftieth day after Passover. Counting the day of Passover itself, Pentecost therefore happened forty-nine days later. That leaves just seven days between the Ascension and Pentecost. So the Holy Spirit fell on the disciples exactly a week after Jesus left them. Why is this significant?

I was baptised in the Spirit five years after I was saved. I said earlier I don't believe this was God's best for me.

The Lord used those forty days to teach the eleven remaining apostles. *On one occasion, while he was eating with them, he gave them this command: "Do not leave Jerusalem, but wait for the gift my Father promised, which you have heard me speak about"* (Acts 1:4).

Luke records it too: *"I am going to send you what my Father has promised; but stay in the city until you have been clothed with power from on high"* (Luke 24:49). As this version is slightly different, it suggests Jesus said it more than once, making sure the disciples got it. It was a command.

Two phrases stand out: *"Stay in the city"* and *"Do not leave Jerusalem"*. We know they only had to wait a week for the Spirit to come. With him came power. Jesus promised that power would enable them to be witnesses, at home and abroad, wherever the Holy Guide led them. The strong implication is that without the Promise of the Father, the power of the disciples was limited.

Applying these verses to ourselves, I believe Jesus is exhorting us to remain in our churches, fellowships, or house groups, until we have been clothed with power from on high. If God thought we needed to be baptised in the Holy Spirit, we need to be. It is, after all, the Lord's idea—no man invented it. Why would we even want to risk being a witness without the Spirit's power?

> If God thought we need to be baptised in the Holy Spirit, we need to be!

Paul's homily on Mars Hill is often touted as an example of a perfect sermon—at the top of his game. Many copy its pattern today. But after Paul's relative failure there, who would want to? F.B. Meyer said, "If Christ waited to be anointed before he went to preach, no young man ought to preach until he, too, has been anointed by the Holy Ghost."

I honour the sacrifice of missionaries throughout the history of the church, going in the strength they have, fighting against insuperable opposition for so long with so little fruit. What would have happened if they had gone, like Paul to Corinth, with a demonstration of the power of the Spirit—prophesying, healing the sick, casting out demons, and raising the dead? We live in such privileged days.

The baptism into the Holy Spirit is God's secret weapon—the intended modus operandi of the church to reach the world. But as we've been saying, this baptism is much more even than that. We're now ready to look at seals. How do they work, and how on earth can the Holy Spirit be a seal?

Chapter 4

The Purpose of Seals

In 2009, Israeli archaeologist, Eilat Mazar, discovered a 2,700-year-old bulla, or clay impression made by a seal, inscribed, "Belonging to Hezekiah, Son of Ahaz, King of Judah" (left picture below). She found the bulla, the size of a thumbnail, in an excavation by the southern wall of the temple mount in Jerusalem.

In the same strata just a few metres away, her team unearthed another bearing the name Isaiah, and underneath, the first three letters, N V Y, of the Hebrew word for prophet (Hebrew reads from right to left). Isaiah was a close adviser to King Hezekiah, influential in the king's success and even prophesying an extra fifteen years of life for him.

LEFT: The bulla of King Hezekiah of Israel   RIGHT: The bulla of Isaiah

Seals have been used by important people and businessmen for over four thousand years, appearing in excavations from Egypt,

Assyria, Babylonia, and ancient Sumeria. Even Abraham could have owned one.

They come in two main forms—cylinder seals, which can be rolled along soft clay to form a picture or inscription; and stamp seals, which are pressed into the clay or wax. Usually made of stone or metal, some are incredibly detailed. Wikipedia says, "In antiquity they were common, largely because they served to authenticate legal documents, such as tax receipts, contracts, wills and decrees." They would often carry more than a signature, revealing much about the person or culture of the day.

Early forms of script such as hieroglyphs and cuneiform were complex, needing time to learn and skill to execute. Few people could read and even fewer, write. However, many could own a seal. Often worn on a string around the neck, they were an everyday item, replacing signatures, photos, passports, passwords and other forms of identification we are familiar with today. How were they used?

Scripture gives a fascinating insight into the process of documentation at the time of Jeremiah. He'd been imprisoned for prophesying that King Zedekiah would be captured by the Babylonians, and Israel taken into exile. Imagine his surprise when the Lord says to him in jail, *Hanamel son of Shallum your uncle is going to come to you and say, "Buy my field at Anathoth, because as nearest relative it is your right and duty to buy it"* (Jeremiah 32:7).

His uncle duly arrived, and Jeremiah weighed out the silver. In the presence of witnesses, he signed two copies of the deed of sale, sealing one. Then told his scribe, Baruch, *"This is what the LORD Almighty, the God of Israel, says: Take these documents, both the sealed and unsealed copies of the deed of purchase, and put them in a clay jar so they will last a long time. For this is what the LORD Almighty, the God of Israel, says: Houses, fields and vineyards will again be bought in this land"* (Jeremiah 32:14-15). The seal was an essential part of the verification process.

To fulfil its purpose therefore, a seal needs to be unique, visible, identifiable, and irreversible. It should also be hard to copy or forge, and long-lasting. All of these characteristics have a significant part to play in our understanding of the seals of the Holy Spirit.

The Sign of the New Covenant

A sign from the Lord always accompanies his covenants and often his promises.

The sign of his covenant with Noah was the rainbow, a symbol of the power and beauty of light after the darkness and destruction of the flood.

When he introduced the Passover, the Lord told the Israelites to paint their doorposts with the blood of the lamb, a symbol of our salvation in Christ. *"The blood will be a sign for you on the houses where you are; and when I see the blood, I will pass over you. No destructive plague will touch you when I strike Egypt"* (Exodus 12:13).

The Sabbath day was the sign of the Old Covenant, in which the Lord's promises were conditional upon their obedience to the Law, which is why the Lord was so angry when they flouted the Sabbath, seeking manna when there was none; keeping it until it stank; and later trading seven days a week. If they could just keep the Sabbath, they would prove their obedience. They couldn't. We can't either.

The covenant sign with Abraham was circumcision, symbolising the separation or holiness of his chosen people, and the intimacy of their relationship.

Perhaps the greatest sign of all was buried in a terse conversation between Isaiah and King Ahaz: *"Therefore the Lord himself will give you a sign: The virgin will be with child and will give birth to a son, and will call him Immanuel"* (Isaiah 7:14). For nothing is impossible with God, as Gabriel reassured the virgin, Mary, seven hundred years later.

So we should expect a sign of the New Covenant too—something unique, identifiable, irreversible.

Communion or the Eucharist, instituted by the Lord Jesus at the last supper, is unique to our faith. A holy sacrament, it's a remembrance of the Lord's death and resurrection. But nowhere is it described as a sign or a seal.

> The baptism with the Holy Spirit is the seal of our salvation

However, Ephesians 1:13-14 tells us, *and you also were included in Christ when you heard the word of truth, the gospel of your salvation. Having believed, you were marked in him with a seal, the promised Holy Spirit, who is a deposit guaranteeing our inheritance until the redemption of those who are God's possession—to the praise of his glory.*

As we've seen, the "promised Holy Spirit" refers to the gift of the Father, and Jesus explained this meant the baptism with the Holy Spirit. This is therefore the seal of our salvation.

It is Unique

We've seen how no one can be baptised with the Spirit unless they are saved. First the blood, then the fire. Therefore no members of other religions can be filled. No atheists, no secularists, no humanists, no one from the New Age. All must first come humbly to the foot of the cross.

No other god can baptise anyone with the Holy Spirit, because the Spirit, with the Father and Son, is the only true God.

Visible

On the day of Pentecost, the holy chaos drew a large crowd. Some mocked. Others were deeply impacted, but no one could ignore the sign.

Later, when Peter preached to Cornelius' Gentile household, the Holy Spirit came on them all. *For they heard them speaking in tongues and praising God* (Acts 10:46).

This puzzled the apostles back in Jerusalem. Peter explained, *"As I began to speak, the Holy Spirit came on them as he had come on us at the beginning. Then I remembered what the Lord had said: 'John baptized with water, but you will be baptized with the Holy Spirit.' So if God gave them the same gift as he gave us, who believed in the Lord Jesus Christ, who was I to think that I could oppose God?"* (Acts 11:15-17). The assembly answered, *"So then, God has granted even the Gentiles repentance unto life"* (Acts 11:18).

Once they began speaking in tongues, the apostles realised they'd been baptised with the Spirit, and once they were baptised with the Spirit, they realised they must be saved. No one <u>thinks</u> they've been baptised with the Spirit. They <u>know</u>.

Identifiable

Speaking in tongues is weird. It's illogical. Why would we want to speak in a language we don't understand? Surely the purpose of language is communication. So why this? Whole books have been written on the reasons, but one of them must be that it identifies those filled with the Spirit.

As soon as we hear another believer speaking in a heavenly language, we feel immediate empathy with them. I have travelled extensively, and wherever I go, I find believers speaking in tongues. Immediately, we are one. Further identification is unnecessary. I don't need to preach the gospel to them. They already know the Lord, because they are baptised with the Holy Spirit.

Irreversible

Once a seal is broken, it cannot be mended. That's the whole point. If it could be removed and restored unblemished, it would be useless.

Now Romans 11:29 says, *for God's gifts and his call are irrevocable.* The promise of the Father is not earned. It is a gift. Therefore it is irrevocable. No one can be un-baptised in the Spirit.

Sadly, however, some do fall away. Hebrews 10:29 warns us of the consequences: *How much more severely do you think a man deserves to be punished who has trampled the Son of God under foot, who has treated as an unholy thing the blood of the covenant that sanctified him, and who has insulted the Spirit of grace?*

These two scriptures appear to be in conflict, but they're not. One who has already *tasted the heavenly gift,* and has *shared in the Holy Spirit* (see Hebrews 6:4), who still has the ability to access his power but refuses to do so, demonstrates beyond doubt his disdain for the Lord. His end is deserved.

Hard to copy

Some years ago, I was ministering to a line of people, when I came to a girl speaking in tongues. It sounded 'normal', but the girl seemed to be striving and stressed. My spirit felt uncomfortable. I sensed the Holy Spirit telling me to rebuke the spirit of the false tongue. I'd never heard of such a thing. What if I was wrong? But I took the plunge and obeyed the Spirit.

Immediately the girl fell to the ground under the Spirit, and became still. Several moments later, she spoke again in tongues, which my spirit sensed was genuine. But this time, a wave of peace washed over her face.

I have since heard several instances of a false tongue. Sometimes people use baby language, perhaps in an environment where there is an expectation to be able to speak in tongues—that isn't a false tongue, but the flesh acting out of pride or embarrassment. The Lord is gracious and understands.

However, the genuine gift is accompanied by the fruits of the Spirit—*love, joy, peace, patience, kindness, goodness, faithfulness, gentleness and self-control* (Galatians 5:22). These the devil cannot copy.

Long-lasting

1 Corinthians 13:8 says, *but where there are prophecies, they will cease; where there are tongues, they will be stilled; where there is knowledge, it will pass away.* Paul is describing the time when we are face to face with the Lord. Then there will be no need of prophecies or other languages. All will be one, and that One will be Christ Jesus.

But until then, tongues <u>will</u> continue, as the definitive sign of the baptism into the Holy Spirit, which is the definitive sign of salvation. For the seven seals of the Spirit are for today, not tomorrow.

And before the perfection comes, the world must face this...

The Seven Seals of Judgement

Seals are one of the great themes of the book of Revelation. However, these are seals of the Lamb not the Spirit. However, there are lessons here before we study those in detail.

Many are convinced, as I am, that we are entering the last seconds of the last days of the prophecies of scripture. Daniel prophesies there will be a seven-year tribulation of the world at the end of the ages, dramatically launched by Jesus himself in Revelation 5.

God the Father produces a scroll, sealed with seven seals. No one is worthy to open them but the Lamb without blemish. As he breaks the seals, he releases a cascade of judgements—war, famine, plague, earthquakes. In the midst of all this horror, we read *then I saw another angel coming up from the east, having the seal of the living God. He called out in a loud voice to the four angels who had been given power to harm the land and the sea: "Do not harm the land or the sea or the trees until we put a seal on the foreheads of the servants of our God"* (Revelation 7:2-3).

These tribulation judgements are designed to cause unbelievers to turn to Christ. Reading between the lines of the story, many millions do repent, but still, tragically, many refuse. The trials become increasingly severe, for the seventh and final seal merely releases further judgements—the seven trumpets sounded by seven angels. And again we read, *they were told not to harm the grass of the earth or any plant or tree, but only those people who did not have the seal of God on their foreheads* (Revelation 9:4).

Christians, we have been marked by a seal, the promised Holy Spirit. Praise God! If this is the Spirit, why the foreheads?

Again, it's unique, visible and identifiable. It also symbolises the humility of those willing to submit their understanding to the will and Word of God.

Now speaking of the rapture, Paul says in 1 Corinthians 15:52 *that in a flash, in the twinkling of an eye, at the last trumpet ... the dead will be raised imperishable, and we will be changed.* If he is referring to the seventh trumpet of Revelation 11, then the rapture occurs at the midpoint of the seven-year tribulation. Against this view, several following passages refer to the saints. However, the tribulation isn't just an outpouring of wrath, but designed to bring millions more into the kingdom of God.

If that's the case, the saints are now unable to proclaim the gospel, which had been their privilege and duty until then. No other person or angel may. But during this dark time, we read, *then I saw another angel flying in midair, and he had the eternal gospel to proclaim to those who live on the earth—to every nation, tribe, language and people* (Revelation 14:6). Even after the church is caught up to be with him, the Father's heart is still for the unbelievers who remain to turn to him. What grace!

But after that, literally all hell breaks loose. Introduce the dragon, the antichrist, and the false prophet. This evil trilogy takes control over the people of the earth, marking their foreheads with <u>his</u> symbol, which is the prelude to the seven bowls of God's wrath, the fall of Babylon, and the final battle of all battles.

Throughout scripture seals are powerful symbols of God's purpose. Let's now look at the seals of the Spirit. What are they, and why are they so important?

Chapter 5

The Seals – Part 1

In the kingdom of God, total transformation needs only seconds.

Stinking of prison, Joseph was washed, shaved, clothed, and marched off to Pharaoh. I doubt he'd been told why, and after his prophecy to the baker, thoughts of execution must have crossed his mind. He was probably beyond caring. But after the Lord gave him the correct interpretations of Pharaoh's dreams, Joseph found the courage to offer detailed advice on how to run Egypt!

Instead of, "Off with his head," Pharaoh asked in Genesis 41:38, *"Can we find anyone like this man, one in whom is the spirit of God?"* Even the pagan king recognised the presence of the Holy Spirit. Pharaoh went on to appoint Joseph as his second-in-command, adding (verse 40), *"Only with respect to the throne will I be greater than you."* This verse is so important we'll return to it.

Meanwhile, the following paragraph describes Joseph's investiture. And it was many years after I'd discovered the seven seals of the Spirit elsewhere in scripture that I realised all seven are here too, detailed in this prophetic passage!

So Pharaoh said to Joseph, "I hereby put you in charge of the whole land of Egypt." Then Pharaoh took his <u>signet ring</u> from his finger and put it on Joseph's finger. He dressed him in <u>robes of fine linen</u> and put a <u>gold chain</u> around his neck. He had him <u>ride in a chariot</u> as his second-in-command, and <u>men shouted</u> before him, "Make way!" Thus he put him in charge of the whole land of Egypt. Then Pharaoh said to Joseph, "I am Pharaoh, but without your word no one will lift hand or foot in all

Egypt." <u>Pharaoh gave Joseph the name Zaphenath-Paneah</u> and <u>gave him Asenath</u> daughter of Potiphera, priest of On, to be his wife. And Joseph went throughout the land of Egypt (Genesis 41:41-45).

Here are seven keys, which prove to be the same seven seals of the Holy Spirit! We'll take them in the order they appear here except for the signet ring, which is so significant it merits its own chapter.

The First Seal—The Seal of Righteousness

First, Pharaoh dressed Joseph in "robes of fine linen".

Robes

Clothing itself is highly symbolic in scripture. Adam and Eve were naked. God removed their inadequate fig leaves and clothed them in animal skins, meaning he was the first to kill. The animals' sacrifice was an atonement—a temporary righteousness until Calvary, where Jesus was crucified, also naked. No atonement for him; he <u>was</u> the atonement.

When High Priest Caiaphas condemned Jesus to death for blasphemy he tore his robes, which was strictly against the Law of Moses, as he well knew: *The high priest ... must not let his hair become unkempt or tear his clothes* (Leviticus 21:10). He tore them in "righteous" indignation, unaware he was symbolising his own unrighteousness in condemning the Righteous One to die.

When David's son Amnon raped his sister, Tamar tore her richly ornamented robe, *"the kind of garment the virgin daughters of the king wore"* (see 2 Samuel 13:18-19). Tearing robes therefore symbolised not merely mourning or grief, but a loss of purity.

When the Prodigal Son returned, his father wrapped the best robe in the house around his pig-muck shoulders. Purity restored!

As children of God, we have been clothed with Christ. *You are all sons of God through faith in Christ Jesus, for all of you who were baptized into Christ have clothed yourselves with Christ* (Galatians 3:26-27). Our own pig-muck shoulders are covered—and not just covered, but made beautiful—by the richly-ornamented robe of <u>his</u> righteousness.

In Isaiah 61, the prophet rejoices: *"I delight greatly in the LORD; my soul rejoices in my God. For he has clothed me with garments of salvation and arrayed me in a robe of righteousness, as a bridegroom adorns his head like a priest, and as a bride adorns herself with her jewels"* (Isaiah 61:10). Isaiah saw a bridal gown, a foretaste of the perfection of the final and greatest wedding of all—the Lamb to his bride, the church, at the end of the age.

Robes signify righteousness. Covering our nakedness and impurity, covering our shame and making us presentable before the Father. Everyone in heaven is clothed.

Fine Linen

The Bible is alive with symbols. Fortunately, it usually reveals their meaning somewhere! This is Revelation 19:6-8:

Then I heard what sounded like a great multitude, like the roar of rushing waters and like loud peals of thunder, shouting:

"Hallelujah! For our Lord God Almighty reigns.

Let us rejoice and be glad and give him glory!

For the wedding of the Lamb has come, and his bride has made herself ready.

Fine linen, bright and clean, was given her to wear."

(Fine linen stands for the righteous acts of the saints.)

But, John, doesn't Isaiah 64:6 say, *"All of us have become like one who is unclean, and all our righteous acts are like filthy rags?"* True, our good deeds can never be called righteous. However, a few chapters earlier, in Revelation 7:14, we read the great multitude had *washed their clothes and made them white in the blood of the Lamb*. So not only have our filthy acts been washed clean by the blood of Jesus, our rags have become fine linen. Oh, the immeasurable grace of God!

Now linen comes from flax, and has been worn for thousands of years. Used in ancient Egypt to shroud mummies, it symbolised light and purity, and was always expensive. Even angels wear it: *Out of the temple came the seven angels with the seven plagues. They were dressed in clean, shining linen and wore golden sashes around their chests* (Revelation 15:6).

Therefore linen also signifies righteousness. Notice again that the fine linen robes were given to the bride, not earned. Her only action was to wash. We receive the righteousness of Jesus by faith in his blood, not by righteous acts.

Everyone John sees in Revelation is not only clothed, but wearing white. After Jesus rose from the dead, he left his earthly clothes in the grave, and returned wearing a new, heavenly set. What we will look like there we don't know, but I think we can guess the colour!

Abraham's righteousness

Remember we discussed earlier (Galatians 3:6) that Abraham believed God and it was credited to him as righteousness? Now, Paul tells us in Romans 4:11, *and he [Abraham] received the sign of circumcision, a <u>seal of the righteousness</u> that he had by faith while he was still uncircumcised. So then, he is the father of all who believe but have not been circumcised, in order that righteousness might be credited to them.*

Abraham was declared righteous because he believed. God needed to give him a seal of his righteousness, so he would always be reminded (several times a day, if you'll excuse me mentioning it) that his righteousness was not of his own making, but a gift from God. Long before the cross, it was a temporary sign until the fulfilment of the Lord's purpose in salvation.

We, therefore, the 'uncircumcised' (not of the flesh, but of the spirit), also need a seal of our righteousness—the baptism of the Holy Spirit. But why is that a seal? Because of the fire.

Holy Fire

Shadrach, Meshach and Abednego were not destroyed in Nebuchadnezzar's furnace. The soldiers were. Why? The burning bush didn't burn up. Why not? When the fire of God fell in Leviticus 9, it consumed the offering, but not the altar, but when the same fire fell on Mount Carmel, it burned up the offering, the stones, the water, everything. Why the difference?

Here's another: When the fire of the Lord consumed Aaron's sons Nadab and Abihu, their cousins carried their remains, *still in their tunics,* outside the camp (see Leviticus 10:5). How could the men be destroyed by fire, but not their tunics?

> The fire of God destroys the unholy and glorifies the holy

The answer came in a flash of revelation. The bush wasn't burnt because it was on holy ground. Shadrach, Meshach and Abednego had just declared their faith that God would save them (therefore were credited righteous). Elijah hadn't consecrated his altar on Mount Carmel, but the one in Leviticus had been. So had Nadab and Abihu's tunics!

The answer is simple, but radical. The fire of God, which is a manifestation of the Holy Spirit, is holy. It destroys anything unholy and glorifies anything deemed to be holy. There are many similar examples in scripture, which I study in greater detail in my book, *Holy Fire* (see Recommended Reading).

As we have seen, the baptism of the Holy Spirit is the symbol of Jesus. *"He will baptise you with the Holy Spirit and with fire,"* declares John the Baptist in Luke 3:16. He goes on to say, *"His winnowing fork is in his hand to clear his threshing floor and to gather the wheat into his barn, but he will burn up the chaff with unquenchable fire"* (Luke 3:17).

A threshing floor was an open space of either packed dirt or levelled rock upon which sheaves were thrashed, either with oxen and a sledge or by hand. The straw was set aside for fodder, leaving the floor covered with a mixture of grain and chaff. This was tossed into the breeze with a large wooden fork with wide tines. The grain would fall to the floor while the chaff drifted away downwind. Psalm 1:4 says the wicked *are like chaff that the wind blows away.*

The images are both powerful and salutary. Threshing is a traumatic business. First the crop is thoroughly smashed, then separated. The good from the bad. The sheep from the goats. So the fire of the Holy Spirit is a separating fire.

But it is more even than that, for the farmer carefully saves the grain and burns the chaff. Not just separated but treated differently. Therefore the Holy Spirit is a discriminating fire, destroying the unholy and glorifying the holy.

Here it is again, this time referring to our works: *If any man builds on this foundation* [Christ] *using gold, silver, costly stones, wood, hay or straw, his work will be shown for what it is, because the Day will bring it to light. It will be revealed with fire, and the fire will test the quality of each man's work. If what he has built survives, he will receive his reward. If it is burned up, he will suffer loss; he himself will be saved, but only as one escaping through the flames* (1 Corinthians 3:12-15).

So the dramatic conclusion is this: If the Holy Spirit fell on the unrighteous he would destroy them. No unbeliever, no atheist, no one from another religion can be baptised with the Spirit. God longs to see them so filled, but his love constrains him, for he doesn't want anyone to perish.

When Jesus promised the baptism with the Holy Spirit he stated, *"The world cannot accept him, because it neither sees him nor knows him. But you know him, for he lives with you and will be in you"* (John 14:17). Now the Greek word translated "accept" is *labein* from the root, *lambano*, a common word which actually means to receive or to take. The world <u>cannot</u> receive the Holy Spirit.

Jesus uses the expression "the world" to mean unbelievers. Of course, they cannot <u>accept</u> the existence and manifestation of the Spirit, because unbelievers cannot understand him. But it's more than that; they cannot <u>receive</u> him either, or they would be destroyed.

No one wants to be the chaff—far better to return to the Rock!

Reassurance

Therefore in order to be baptised with the Spirit, the Lord must first give us the gift of righteousness. Remember—first the blood, then the fire (the Spirit), then the smoke (the glory). And it cannot be by works, or it would be wages.

So the Lord designed righteousness to be credited to us by faith in the death and resurrection of Jesus. *For in the gospel a righteousness from God is revealed, a righteousness that is by faith from first to last, just as it is written: "The righteous will live by faith"* (Romans 1:17). And the righteousness we receive is his, not ours: *God made him who had no sin to be sin for us, so that in him we might become the <u>righteousness of God</u>* (2 Corinthians 5:21). That is how righteous we are in God's sight. If God is our Father, how can we not be like him? We are adopted into a very righteous Family.

And since the fire of God discriminates between the holy and unholy, once we have been deemed to be righteous by faith in the blood of Jesus, we can expect to be glorified. At Pentecost, individual flames, one for every head, fell on each disciple. They were instantly changed, and the fire filled their spirits. Even John the Baptist didn't anticipate this. He'd prophesied the destruction, but not the transformed lives.

We'd seen a glimpse of it when Samuel prophesied over Saul, *"The Spirit of the LORD will come upon you in power... and you will be changed into a different person"* (1 Samuel 10:6). We'd caught a whiff of its nation-changing potential when the pillar of fire guided and protected the Israelites as they trembled, waiting to escape the Egyptian army.

But here were one hundred and twenty men and women (and who's to say there were no children present) baptised with the Holy Spirit, willing and ready to change the world. They did. Today hundreds of millions of Christians are baptised with the Spirit. Millions are coming to Christ and millions being healed under their hands.

But the immediate result was a disturbance. The crowd mocked their tongue-speaking. "They're drunk!" They've been mocking ever since. The enemy hates it.

Once we understand this, we realise how the seal works. Whenever we are tempted by the devil to think we may not be saved (perhaps he's manipulated us into doing something we regret and we went along with the programme), we need only declare, "I am saved. I am filled with the Spirit. And I couldn't be if I wasn't saved."

If the devil continues the conversation, saying, "But you're not filled with the Spirit," we only have to start speaking in tongues.

"Devil, I couldn't speak in tongues unless I was baptised with the Holy Spirit, and I couldn't be baptised with the Spirit unless I was saved. So get behind me!"

This seal of our righteousness before God gives us wonderful reassurance of our relationship with him. The Lord knows there are many times we feel inadequate, unholy, and ill-equipped to do his work. Abraham had only to go to the bathroom. We merely need to speak in tongues to be totally confident we are righteous in his sight.

> The baptism of the Holy Spirit guarantees your righteousness in God's sight. You are sealed!

The High Priest's Seal

Part of the clothing of the High Priest was his turban. Exodus 28:36-38 tells us, *"Make a plate of pure gold and engrave on it as on a seal: HOLY TO THE LORD. Fasten a blue cord to it to attach it to the turban; it is to be on the front of the turban. It will be on Aaron's forehead, and he will bear the guilt involved in the sacred gifts the Israelites consecrate, whatever their gifts may be. It will be on Aaron's forehead continually so that they will be <u>acceptable to the LORD</u>.*

The seal symbolises the purity of our own High Priest, the Lord Jesus who bears our guilt. And as we inherit his righteousness, these scriptures tell us we are therefore also holy in the Lord's sight. We are acceptable to the Lord. Continually. Hallelujah!

This too is why the saints in the time of the tribulation receive the seal of the Lord on their foreheads, just as Aaron did—identifiable, visible, unalterable. Holy.

The baptism of the Holy Spirit is a seal on your forehead:

HOLY TO THE LORD. It <u>guarantees</u> your righteousness in God's sight. Sealed!

Faith

As an ex-farmer, I am a practical man. I find theory for its own sake tiresome. I like things to work. So I love how the Lord has given us such clear evidence of his salvation. Tongues may seem strange, but they are unique for a reason—a concrete sign of our righteousness. They have to be created by the Spirit. Apparently, research shows the language part of our brain is inactive when we speak in tongues.

Now faith is the substance of things hoped for, the evidence of things not seen (Hebrews 11:1 KJV). We cannot see God. We cannot feel our salvation. We receive them by faith, that is, we trust the Lord to fulfil his promises.

But in order to make our hope more certain, the Lord has given us this sign. Therefore the purpose of the seal of righteousness is to encourage our faith. With this new confidence in his astonishing gift of righteousness, we can step with confidence into the ministry he has for us. *Stand firm then… with the breastplate of righteousness in place* (Ephesians 6:14). The breastplate covers our heart, symbolising our life and our passion. It also covers our breath—the same word for spirit in Hebrew.

Thank you, Lord!

The Second Seal—The Seal of Proof

Firstly, Pharaoh dressed Joseph in a robe of fine linen. Righteousness must come first or we perish. Next, he placed a gold chain around his neck. Why?

Gold chains, known as mayoral livery, have long been worn in

England as a symbol of office. If ten officials entered a room, one wearing the gold chain, we would know the mayor at once. The tradition apparently began six hundred years ago, but it's been around a lot longer than that.

In 539 BC, King Belshazzar of Babylon and his one thousand guests filled goblets from the Lord's temple with wine and toasted the gods of gold and silver. Suddenly, ghostly fingers appeared, writing on the wall. Swooning in fear, *the king called out for the enchanters, astrologers and diviners to be brought and said to these wise men of Babylon, "Whoever reads this writing and tells me what it means will be clothed in purple and have a gold chain placed around his neck, and he will be made the third highest ruler in the kingdom"* (Daniel 5:7). The Prophet Daniel duly appeared, interpreted the writing and refused the gifts.

So Pharaoh's offer of a gold chain to Joseph wasn't exclusive to Egyptian culture. Again, the gold chain was unique, recognisable, and immediately identified the holder with his office. As soon as people saw the chain, they knew to submit to his authority. Uniform is the symbol of office of the police. Their cars are clearly identified since only police drive them. As soon as we see the colours, we slow down!

When Jeremiah bought his uncle's field (Jeremiah 32), they made two identical copies of the deed of sale, signed both together with witnesses, sealed one copy, and stored them safely. Should anyone suspect fraud, he could break the seal and verify the copy and signatures. The seal was the proof the visible copy was original and genuine.

After the exiles had returned to Jerusalem, they made a solemn agreement with the Lord to keep his commands, binding themselves with a curse and an oath. *"In view of all this, we are making a binding agreement, putting it in writing, and our leaders, our*

Levites and our priests are affixing their seals to it" (Nehemiah 9:38). These seals proved their sincerity and commitment to the agreement.

Not the least of the Apostle Paul's trials was his struggle for recognition of his call. *"Am I not free?"* he writes to the Corinthians. *"Am I not an apostle? Have I not seen Jesus our Lord? Are you not the result of my work in the Lord? Even though I may not be an apostle to others, surely I am to you! For you are the seal of my apostleship in the Lord"* (1 Corinthians 9:1-2). The very fact of their existence was proof Paul had established the church among them, and was therefore an apostle. Had he not visited them, they would still be dead in their sins. And if they are the proof of his apostleship, how much more is the baptism with the Spirit the proof of the Lord's favour and grace toward us? The Lord said, "I will build my church." We are marked with his seal.

Our lives today are swamped by the need for passwords—proof of who we are. (We even use passwords to access our passwords.) In more godly days, newly-weds couldn't book a double room in a respectable hotel without their marriage certificate, proof that their relationship was genuine. The baptism with the Holy Spirit is the proof of our relationship with the Lord—original, real, and genuine. What's more, it's proof of the Lord's own sincerity and commitment to his children.

Against all his traditions, Peter obeyed the Lord and for the first time in his life entered the house of a Gentile, Cornelius. He must have prickled with embarrassment. But while he was still preaching, the whole gathering (rudely!) began speaking in tongues. Therefore they'd received the baptism of the Holy Spirit. Therefore they were saved. *The circumcised believers who had come with Peter were astonished that the gift of the Holy Spirit had been poured out even on the Gentiles* (Acts 10:45).

And if I find myself among strangers in another church or another country, I only have to listen for those speaking or praying in tongues to know they too are baptised with the Holy Spirit. They too are saved, and therefore my brothers and sisters in the Lord.

For the same reasons that the fire of God would destroy the unrighteous, the baptism with the Spirit is the seal of the proof of my salvation, stamped by the Lord himself. Praise his wonderful Name!

Encouragement

In a world of lies, we all need reassurance of truth. We hear the spin, but how can we know it's genuine?

Jesus said there would be many false messiahs, just as there are many false prophets and false religions. *"By their fruit you will recognise them,"* Jesus said in Matthew 7:20. Not by their fine words, or talents, or riches or smart clothes. How many times did he say, "Watch out?" If we need to be reminded so often, the risk of deception is real. *But the fruit of the Spirit is love, joy, peace, patience, kindness, goodness, faithfulness, gentleness and self-control. Against such things there is no law* (Galatians 5:22-23).

The purpose of the seal of proof is the encouragement of the saints. *Then the church throughout Judea, Galilee and Samaria enjoyed a time of peace. It was strengthened; and <u>encouraged by the Holy Spirit</u>, it grew in numbers, living in the fear of the Lord* (Acts 9:31).

The baptism with the Holy Spirit is our gold chain of office, the symbol to both the saved and unsaved, who we belong to and whom we serve. We are his.

The Third Seal—The Seal of Security

Egyptologist Howard Carter had been searching for Tutenkhamun's tomb for years. In 1922, digging in yet another site in Egypt's Valley of the Kings, he came across a closed, double door. Its iron handles were tied with rope, and sealed with a clay seal bearing hieroglyphs, which cursed anyone tampering with the grave.

It was later discovered the tomb had been robbed not long after the death of the Pharaoh, then hurriedly re-sealed by officials to prevent further desecration. That seal had remained, unbroken, for 3,245 years.

Pharaoh's third act in elevating Joseph as his second-in-command was to have him ride in a royal chariot. Most Egyptian chariots were war machines—the tanks of their day. A little like a modern-day sulky, they were drawn by two horses and usually manned by a charioteer and an archer. In the days before cavalry, they were fast, effective, and greatly feared.

But they required imported materials and skill to construct. So only the rich could afford them, making them a status symbol of wealth and success. (What has changed?) Those of kings and princes were often overlaid in silver, gold, or electrum, a mixture of the two metals. Royal chariots were elaborately decorated and wider, with room enough for an extra man.

No doubt when Joseph rose to power so rapidly, other high-ranking officials felt both jealous and threatened. So when Pharaoh had Joseph ride in one of his chariots, he was not only greatly honouring the former slave, he was giving him his own private security team. Chariots were a symbol of security—another purpose for the seal of the Spirit.

And Pharaoh wasn't the only one with chariots.

Chariots of fire

Elisha the prophet lived in the northern part of divided Israel, under the rule of apostate kings who were at war with Aram. The Aramean king, Ben-Hadad, accused his cabinet of spying for Israel.

One of his officers explained. *"Elisha, the prophet who is in Israel, tells the king of Israel the very words you speak in your bedroom"* (2 Kings 6:12).

Thinking he could use such a valuable informant, Ben-Hadad commanded, "Capture him!" Some nights later his army surrounded the city where Elisha was staying.

Arising at dawn, the prophet's servant saw the Aramean army. *"Oh, my lord, what shall we do?"*

Elisha had already seen the Lord's security forces in the Jordan valley, when a chariot and horses of fire suddenly appeared and caught up Elijah to heaven. So he reassured his servant. *"Don't be afraid... those who are with us are more than those who are with them." And Elisha prayed, "O LORD, open his eyes so he may see." Then the LORD opened the servant's eyes, and he looked and saw the hills full of horses and chariots of fire all around Elisha* (2 Kings 6:16-17).

Revelation 12:4 implies that one third of the angels fell with satan. If that is so, two thirds remain faithful to the Lord, outnumbering the demons two to one! So we too can say <u>those with us are more than with them.</u> More than that, fire is a symbol of the Holy Spirit. We also have chariots of fire—the Holy Spirit!

So chariots represent security. "Don't be afraid," Elisha said. How does this fit with seals?

Maintaining the status quo

The death of Jesus caused the Pharisees almost as much angst as his life. They went to Pilate. *"Sir," they said, "we remember that while he was still alive that deceiver said, 'After three days I will rise again.' So give the order for the tomb to be made secure until the third day. Otherwise, his disciples may come and steal the body and tell the people that he has been raised from the dead. This last deception will be worse than the first."*

"*Take a guard,*" *Pilate answered.* "*Go, make the tomb as secure as you know how.*"

So they went and made the tomb secure by putting a seal on the stone and posting the guard (Matthew 27:63-66).

Pilate's brevity reeks of his frustration! However, the most secure ways they knew to prevent anyone removing the body were to post a guard and put a seal on the stone. It would be immediately clear if anyone had moved it.

That didn't trouble the angel of the Lord, who, in Matthew's version (28:2), *came down from heaven, and, going to the tomb, rolled back the stone* [perhaps with a flick of his wrist] *and sat on it.* The guards collapsed in a dead faint. But Jesus didn't walk out alive; he was already gone. Hallelujah! The stone was not rolled away for him to escape, but for us to find it empty. But notice: The seal secured the tomb.

This story has a prophetic foretaste in the Old Testament. During the Israelites' exile in Babylon, King Darius' satraps were jealous of the Prophet Daniel and plotted his demise. They invented grounds to execute Daniel by manipulating Darius into passing a law to worship only the king. As expected, Daniel refused to obey. The king reluctantly allowed them to throw Daniel into the lion's den.

A stone was brought and placed over the mouth of the den, and the king sealed it with his own signet ring and with the rings of his nobles, so that Daniel's situation might not be changed (Daniel 6:17).

Notice the stone, the seals, and the key phrase, *so that Daniel's situation might not be changed.*

Therefore, security is another purpose of seals. In all these stories, seals were used to ensure the status quo. Mumbai Customs sealed my video projector to ensure no one tampered with the box—perhaps by stealing the projector and leaving the box behind. Their seal prevented any thoughts of theft. It worked!

Why, then, do we need a seal of security for our salvation?

Once saved, always saved?

This is a popular position in some Christian circles. The idea is that once we've believed in Christ, we cannot backslide. If we do, the argument goes, we weren't saved in the first place. However, it follows the path of many false doctrines—taking a few scriptures out of context, and ignoring the many against it.

When we believe in the Lord Jesus and his substitutionary death, we are born again, become new creations, and *have crossed over from death to life* (John 5:24). These concepts suggest irreversible change.

Furthermore, Jesus said, *I give them eternal life, and they shall never perish; no one can snatch them out of my hand* (John 10:28). People have therefore concluded that once we are saved, we are always saved.

But concluding we can therefore never backslide misses the main point—we still have the free will to walk out of the Lord's hand by ourselves. We cannot be snatched out by others or even by the devil. But we can certainly <u>choose</u> to leave. The Lord never removes our free will because he wants our love and love is a choice. (Incidentally, it also means we cannot blame the devil if we backslide. No, that's our own fault.)

The once-saved-always-saved doctrine is dangerous because it becomes a licence to live ungodly or uncommitted lives. Furthermore, the doctrine says if we continue to live in sin then we weren't saved in the first place. However, if we have had a genuine encounter with the Lord, made a firm commitment, and then fallen away, how can we know that any further repentance is genuine? Or will we still not be "properly saved"? So, ironically, this false teaching is much less secure than the truth—that we can fall away! Being aware we can all fall away causes us to live in holy fear of the Lord, determined to stay strong.

A friend once said to his pastor, "I don't need to worry. I'll never be unfaithful to my wife."

The pastor rebuked him. "Don't ever say such a thing! We can all be tempted. Are you more godly than King David?"

My friend got the point. For there are literally dozens of scriptures which make it clear we can backslide and lose our salvation. It is a main theme of the book of Hebrews. I will share just three scriptures.

In one of the classic gospel passages (1 Corinthians 15:2), Paul declares, *by this gospel you are saved, if you hold firmly to the word I preached to you. Otherwise, you have believed in vain.*

Jesus, likewise, speaking of remaining in the vine, says, *"If anyone does not remain in me, he is like a branch that is thrown away and withers; such branches are picked up, thrown into the fire and burned"* (John 15:6). That's pretty clear.

Speaking of Israel, Paul uses the metaphor of olive trees. *For if God did not spare the natural branches, he will not spare you either. Consider therefore the kindness and sternness of God: sternness to those who fell, but kindness to you, provided that you continue in his kindness. Otherwise, you also will be cut off* (Romans 11:21-22).

Notice the conditions, "if" and "provided that", and the very clear alternatives. Read the New Testament again beginning with Hebrews and mark this theme. It's everywhere.

It's a common fallacy that God's grace and his love are

unconditional. All the promises of the Old Testament are conditional upon obedience to the Law. If we obey him, he will keep his promises. But the Old Testament is there to prove we are unable to keep God's commands! So he cut a New Covenant, this time with Jesus, and we believers are the beneficiaries. But it is still conditional. However the condition has changed from obedience to faith. His promises are ours *if* we believe.

Writing to the Corinthians about maintaining their faith in Christ, Paul says, *for no matter how many promises God has made, they are "Yes" in Christ. And so through him the "Amen" is spoken by us to the glory of God* (2 Corinthians 1:20). The word, *amen*, means *"let it be so"*. If we say "Amen", it means we agree. We believe. Therefore the promises are ours when, but only when, we say "Yes" to Christ and believe. Salvation is ours by faith. If we stop believing, we are no longer believers. Unbelievers are not saved.

> The Lord has given us a seal of security, so that our situation may not be changed

This is both very simple and yet profound truth.

And the demonstration of genuine faith? Obedience, which now becomes possible because it comes from hearts of flesh, directed by the Holy Spirit. But, again, the Lord never removes our free will—free to follow or free to fall.

Backsliding doesn't mean we have sinned somewhere along the road—it means no longer believing in Christ. We all sin (see 1 John 1:8), but as believers, we know our sin is paid for by the blood of Christ. We confess (verse 9) and he will forgive us, and purify us from all unrighteousness. However, if we no longer believe, we have nowhere to go. The sin remains.

Therefore the Lord has given us a seal of security—the promised Holy Spirit, so that our situation may not be changed! In fact, this would be pointless if our situation was irreversible. It only makes sense because backsliding is a real possibility. If the Lord's tomb could never be opened, there was no need for guards and a seal. If there were no thieves in India, Customs didn't need to seal my package.

God has given us the baptism of the Holy Spirit as a seal of the security of our salvation, so that our situation, like Daniel's, may not be changed. God's purpose is to make backsliding so much harder, without removing our free will. We have, as Hebrews 6:4-5 reminds us, been enlightened by the truth of Christ; tasted the heavenly gift of salvation; shared in the baptism of the Holy Spirit; and tasted the goodness of the word of God and the powers of the coming age.

We are sealed. We are secure—safe in his everlasting arms and in the knowledge that he himself will never let us go, unless we choose to walk away. What a wonderful Saviour!

Perseverance

Now we know that, we have the courage to push through the tough times.

After Bron and I left Christ for All Nations, we began our own ministry. We'd experienced the spiritual highs of Reinhard Bonnke's crusades, seeing millions come to Christ. As his representative, I'd also been invited to speak in many well-known churches around the world. But we were exhausted, and the Lord prompted us to leave.

Naively, we expected to launch a great ship. Instead, we pastored a tiny church for a couple of years, started a charity, and preached on occasion to crowds of a few hundred in Indian villages. Many times the devil said we'd made a bad mistake. We'd tasted honey. What was this?

After three years, we were desperate to know what the Lord wanted us to do, and where. So we attended a prophecy day for about one hundred people. The main speaker said he'd invited a prophetess from Ireland, who may have a few words for us. She knew no one.

Sure enough, at the morning break she stood and said, "I think there's someone here called Fergusson. Something to do with farming." (I had been a farmer.) She then accurately described the clothes I was wearing. The friends we'd come with were already chuckling.

She continued, "You've been worshiping with the multitudes." Two weeks earlier we'd been in Lagos, Nigeria, in front of a crowd of 1.6 million.

"I have this word, 'Adeboye.'" We'd sat next to him on the platform in Nigeria. She then followed with something about Psalm 23 and sat down.

I had never in my life heard such accurate words of knowledge. But there seemed to be no direction at all! I confess, at lunchtime I rushed outside to be alone with God. "Lord," I almost shouted, "what was that about? We want to know what you want us to do!"

As clearly as I've ever heard him speak, he replied, "John, I have your name and address. I can call you any time I want." Reassurance flooded my soul. Okay! I could live with that. I could persevere, because the Lord's got it all in hand. Some years later he led us to New Zealand and a new phase of our lives.

More recently I have realised Psalm 23 speaks of the Lord's promise to guide us always, both on the mountaintops and in the valleys. We'd surely experienced both! And I can honestly declare he has kept his word: *Surely goodness and love will follow me all the days of my life, and I will dwell in the house of the LORD forever* (Psalm

23:6).

An understanding of our security in Christ develops perseverance.

~ ✠ ~

The Holy Spirit is given for much more than power. He is the seal of our righteousness, because without the blood, the fire would destroy us. This gives us faith to stand against all the wiles of the enemy, because we <u>know</u> we are saved, because we <u>know</u> we are baptised with the Holy Spirit, because we have his power and can speak in tongues.

He is the seal of proof, because the Spirit guarantees that it is the Lord who has saved us, and not we ourselves. This gives us encouragement when the Lord appears to be distant. He saved us—how can he not be with us?

And he is the seal of our security, so that our situation may not be changed. If it was impossible for us to backslide, the seal of security is pointless. However, with his power and his guidance, he will keep us safe in the everlasting arms.

These are wonderful, but they are less than half the story. The other seals are even more amazing.

Chapter 6

The Seals – Part 2

The seven seals of the Holy Spirit are given to us for our comfort and security. But the Lord has much more in store.

First, he gives us the baptism with the Holy Spirit as a seal of our righteousness before him—the righteousness of Jesus himself. Pharaoh dressed Joseph in robes of fine linen.

Second, he gives us a seal of proof—that we are in a covenant relationship with him. The baptism with the Spirit is our marriage certificate. Evidence. Pharaoh hung a gold chain around Joseph's neck as a symbol of his new status, his badge of office.

> The baptism with the Holy Spirit is our marriage certificate

Third, like Pharaoh, the Lord allows us to ride in his own chariot! He gives us his own security team, his angels (Hebrews 1:14): *Are not all angels ministering spirits sent to serve those who will inherit salvation?* Believers baptised in the Holy Spirit are less prone to fall. The Spirit is given so that our situation may not be changed.

In this chapter we study a further three seals for our encouragement, obedience and hope.

The Fourth Seal—The Seal of Approval

Here is Joseph's inauguration again:

> So Pharaoh said to Joseph, "I hereby put you in charge of the whole land of Egypt." Then Pharaoh took his <u>signet ring</u> from his finger and put it on Joseph's finger. He dressed him in <u>robes of fine linen</u> and put a <u>gold chain</u> around his neck. He had him <u>ride in a chariot</u> as his second-in-command, and <u>men shouted</u> before him, "Make way!" Thus he put him in charge of the whole land of Egypt. Then Pharaoh said to Joseph, "I am Pharaoh, but without your word no one will lift hand or foot in all Egypt." <u>Pharaoh gave Joseph the name Zaphenath-Paneah</u> and <u>gave him Asenath</u> daughter of Potiphera, priest of On, to be his wife. And Joseph went throughout the land of Egypt (Genesis 41:41-45).

After Pharaoh had given Joseph his own chariot, we read, *men shouted before him, "Make Way!"*

Weaving a chariot and horses through the throngs in the Egyptian market-place would have been impossible. There were no traffic signals. So road-clearing slaves ran ahead of the chariots and litters of important people, shouting "Make way!" and no doubt waving sticks. The crowd did the same for Jesus as he rode up to Jerusalem before he died.

The Lord makes a way for us where there is no way. In 1992, Jamaican pastors invited Reinhard Bonnke to hold a crusade in Kingston, its capital. Jamaica was well off Bonnke's radar, so as the International Crusade Director I was despatched to check it out. I met with several leaders. Some were keen, others indifferent. I remained unconvinced until someone suggested I visit a village in the mountains.

In my rental car, I twisted through the jungly hills until I came to a small Methodist church. Thinking I was on wild goose chase, I knocked reluctantly on the door.

The pastor eyed this strange white man. "Yes? What can I do for you?"

"I am John Fergusson. I have come from Reinhard Bonnke."

The pastor burst into tears, hugging me like family. "Praise the Lord! I have been praying for five years for someone to come from Christ for all Nations. Praise the Lord!"

Needless to say, we held a great crusade in Jamaica the next year, with many thousands saved.

But making a way isn't the only reason for the call. The slaves ran ahead of Joseph because he had been appointed as Pharaoh's representative. It was a sign of his approval.

God approves the Gentiles too

Praying on the roof of Simon the tanner, the Apostle Peter had a vision. It changed his life, and ours! Three times the Lord encouraged him to eat unclean things. Facing a classic clash of cultures, Peter must have felt sick. "Surely not, Lord!"

Let's look at this story again. By God's grace, Peter obeyed the Spirit rather than his stomach, and headed north to the house of Cornelius, a Roman centurion and a Gentile.

In our egalitarian world, it's hard for us to imagine the challenge. Peter had never entered a Gentile home in his life. Was he expecting the fire of God's judgement to fall, like Nadab and Abihu? But the Spirit had told him to come, so in trepidation he preached the gospel.

While Peter was still speaking these words, the Holy Spirit came on all who heard the message. The circumcised believers who had come with Peter were astonished that the gift of the Holy Spirit had been poured out even on the Gentiles. For they heard them speaking in tongues and praising God (Acts 10:44-46).

But when Peter returned to Jerusalem some of his brethren

were outraged. *"You went into the house of uncircumcised men and ate with them!"*

He recounted all that had happened, concluding, *"So if God gave them the same gift as he gave us, who believed in the Lord Jesus Christ, who was I to think that I could oppose God?"* (Acts 11:17). When they heard this, they had no further objections and praised God.

Later in Acts 15:8, Peter said, *"God, who knows the heart, showed that <u>he accepted them</u> by giving the Holy Spirit to them, just as he did to us."*

The Lord accepted Cornelius and his family because they believed the gospel Peter preached, *that everyone who believes in Jesus receives forgiveness of sins through his name* (Acts 10:43). In fact, the Spirit fell on them as Peter spoke those very words. At the moment they believed, their hearts changed, and the Lord placed on them all his seal of acceptance, the precious Holy Spirit.

And as we have seen, it's impossible to receive the Spirit unless we are saved. Peter knew this, and immediately ordered they be baptised in the name of Jesus Christ.

The same had happened for Jesus himself. When John baptised him in the Jordan, Jesus rose from the water, *and the Holy Spirit descended on him in bodily form like a dove. And a voice came from heaven: "You are my Son, whom I love; with you I am well pleased"* (Luke 3:22).

No one else received this divine accolade—<u>well</u> pleased. The Father affirmed Jesus twice, here at his baptism and again at his transfiguration. And how did God seal the voice from heaven? By sending the Spirit! Jesus later said about himself, *"On him God the Father has placed his seal of approval"* (John 6:27).

Approval is greater than acceptance. We can accept to live under laws we dislike, because our governments have passed them. We can accept people into our fellowships as a "work in progress", but we don't approve of some of their behaviour!

But the Lord goes further—the Spirit is his seal of approval. What does this imply?

Divine quality control

We are all familiar with them. The product reaches the end of the assembly line and is tested. Does it work? Is it safe? Does it meet the manufacturer's high standards? If it passes, it is stamped with a mark.

The ASQ website (www.asq.org) tells us, "The quality movement can trace its roots back to medieval Europe, where craftsmen began organizing into unions called guilds in the late 13th century. These guilds were responsible for developing strict rules for product and service quality. Inspection committees enforced the rules by marking flawless goods with a special mark or symbol."

But the Lord was onto it first: *And you also were included in Christ when you heard the word of truth, the gospel of your salvation. Having believed, you were marked in him with a seal, the promised Holy Spirit* (Ephesians 1:13).

The purpose of such marks is to reassure the consumer that the product is both genuine and of good quality. The Lord marks us with his Spirit, to prove we are his, that our salvation is real (we are not destroyed), and we pass the righteousness test! (Not our own righteousness, of course, but the Lord's.)

The Father has placed on you his seal of his approval. You are marked. You pass divine quality control! But notice again the order of events: "Having believed" comes first.

We are loved, with a divine, four-dimensional, incomprehensible love. Six times the Apostle John refers to himself as 'the disciple whom Jesus loved' (e.g. John 13:23). I used to think that was pretty arrogant. Didn't Jesus love the others too? What made John so special? But I came to realise the Lord had given John a revelation of the extent of the Father's love for us.

> Put your own name here, and say aloud:
> "_____,
> the disciple whom Jesus loves."

So we can say the same of ourselves. Fill in the box and declare it!

The baptism with the Holy Spirit is a seal of God's approval of us, but not because we are good. No, no, no. Cornelius's household had only been believers for seconds, and I don't doubt there were some rat-bags among them! The seal of approval is because we believe.

(And if you have persevered this far, but haven't yet believed, then pause now and thank God that Jesus Christ has taken away your sins, and declare, "Jesus is Lord!")

The Fifth Seal—The Seal of Ownership

Now it is God who makes both us and you stand firm in Christ. He anointed us, set his seal of ownership on us, and put his Spirit in our hearts as a deposit, guaranteeing what is to come (2 Corinthians 1:21-22).

I attended boarding schools throughout my early years. All my belongings had to be marked with my name and number, either with indelible ink or tags, lovingly sewn on by my mother. If you lived in any such institution, I am sure you remember your number.

Belonging has two imperatives—whose we are, and whose we are not!

It has become a cliché that it takes a village to raise a child. But wired deep into our spirits by our heavenly Father are the needs to love and be loved, to know and be known, and to belong. Perverted belonging descends into tribalism, nationalism, racism and war. But in the Lord's hands (whether acknowledged or not) it yields family, community and brotherhood. We were designed to be owned, and everyone belongs to somebody!

Whose we aren't

First of all, as believers in Christ, we are not our own. *Do you not know that your body is a temple of the Holy Spirit, who is in you, whom you have received from God? <u>You are not your own; you were bought at a price</u>. Therefore honour God with your body* (1 Corinthians 6:19-20).

When we gave our life to Christ, ownership changed hands. Jesus now has the keys. But too many of us want to keep part back for themselves! Reinhard Bonnke tells the following story:

A man gave his house to Jesus. He said, "You are now the owner of my house. Please feel free to use the master bedroom."

"Thank you," the Lord said.

But that night a terrible knocking came from the front door. The man rose to answer. There was the devil! Before he could shut the door, the devil invaded, and they fought the whole night. Exhausted, the man finally evicted him.

When Jesus came down for breakfast, the man said, "Where were you? I have been fighting the devil all night."

"Well," said Jesus, "you only gave me one room of your house."

"Oh, forgive me. Please, have the whole top floor."

"Thank you," the Lord said.

The next night the terrible knocking came again, and another all-night fight ensued. At breakfast the man cried, "Jesus, why didn't you help me?"

"Well," said Jesus, "you only gave me the top floor."

"Forgive me, Lord. Here are the keys to the whole house."

Jesus smiled. "Thank you, my friend."

The knocking came once more and the man got up to answer. But he heard firm footsteps on the stairs. Jesus threw open the front door. The devil stood there.

"Yes? What do you want?" said Jesus.

The devil bowed low. "Oh," he said, "I must have the wrong house."

Selah.

> There is no kingdom of grey

We are not the devil's either. To those who refused to believe in him, Jesus said, *"You belong to your father, the devil, and you want to carry out your father's desire"* (John 8:44a).

There are only two spiritual kingdoms—light and darkness. We are either in one or the other; there is no kingdom of grey. Jesus said to Paul (Acts 26:17b-18), *"I am sending you to [the Gentiles] to open their eyes and turn them from darkness to light, and from the power of Satan to God."* If we are not in the kingdom of light, we are in the kingdom of darkness. Colossians says we have been *rescued from the dominion of darkness and brought into the kingdom of the Son* (Colossians 1:13). If we are in the dominion of darkness, we follow the way of the world, and belong to the devil.

Whose we are

But thank God for his grace! If we gave our lives to him, we now belong to God. *If we live, we live to the Lord; and if we die, we die to the Lord. So, whether we live or die, we belong to the Lord* (Romans 14:8). We were slaves to sin, trapped and manipulated by the enemy. But we are now slaves of righteousness. Owned, yes, but owned for good, and not for evil.

Therefore Lord Jesus has set on us his seal of ownership. *Having believed, you were marked in him with a seal, the promised Holy Spirit, who is a deposit guaranteeing our inheritance until the redemption of those who are God's possession—to the praise of his glory* (Ephesians 1:13b-14).

Once again, the baptism in the Holy Spirit proves we belong to him. No devil can fill us with the Spirit. Nor can the world. They do not even understand the Spirit.

We belong to the Lord. He paid for us. We are his! We don't belong to another organisation or another god. We don't even belong to a church, a denomination or even to the church. We are the church and belong to Christ. We are his bride.

However, when we look again at the parallel story of Pharaoh appointing Joseph, the seal of ownership isn't so clear. Allow me a short diversion.

The authority of naming

If you have a new baby, you have the right to name your child. You don't expect a stranger to walk up and say, "You will call your child Jane." No, the child is under your authority.

In scripture, to name something or someone demonstrates authority over that person or thing. God named the sun and moon, the light and darkness. He named the stars (see Psalm 147:4). But when he placed Adam in the Garden of Eden, he brought the animals to Adam to name. Why? Because he had just given him authority over them in Chapter 1. Therefore they were Adam's to name, not God's.

When God made a covenant with Abram, he changed his name to Abraham. When the Lord wrestled with Jacob, he renamed him Israel. Both new names represented what they would become, and no longer be what they had been.

In Revelation 2:17 we read, *"To him who overcomes, I will give some of the hidden manna. I will also give him a white stone with a new name written on it, known only to him who receives it."* You have a unique name, known only to you and the Lord Jesus. And he will also write on you his own new name (see Revelation 3:12). Naming is important to God.

Now when Pharaoh appointed Joseph, we read, *Pharaoh gave Joseph the name Zaphenath-Paneah* (Genesis 41:45a). By this, Pharaoh was demonstrating his authority over Joseph, but at the same time renamed him to reflect his future, not his past.

According to the International Standard Bible Encyclopaedia Online, Zaphenath-Paneah means, "the one who furnishes the nourishment of life". Pharaoh's focus was probably the grain Joseph would collect and distribute. But the parallels with the Holy Spirit are striking. It is through the Spirit we live, and by him we minister the bread of life, the Lord Jesus.

We have also been renamed after our Saviour. "The Christ" means "The Anointed One", that is, full of the Holy Spirit. We are called "Christians" because we also have the Spirit, and because we are under a new authority. We are renamed according to our destiny, not our past!

The purpose: Obedience

As Christians, Jesus Christ is our Lord. We submit to him our wills, our bodies, our spirits—our whole lives. He is ours and we are his. We resign our own agendas, even our thinking, so that we are able to fulfil his purpose for us.

Watchman Nee said, "The greatest demand God has made on man is not bearing the cross, offerings, consecration or self-sacrifice. God's greatest demand on man is submission." Is he really our King? Is he really Lord of our life?

To submit requires more than simple obedience—because we can obey through gritted teeth. If we are truly submitted, we rejoice in obeying our Lord because we know it pleases him. And it will be God's best plan for our own lives, for others, and for the world. Obeying becomes not only a great privilege, but our greatest pleasure.

If the queen of England visited our home and asked, "John, would you do something for us?" Not only would I jump to obey, I would glow with the satisfaction that the <u>queen</u> had asked <u>me</u> to do her a service. And probably bore my friends with the tale for years.

Why then do we find obedience to the Lord so difficult? It is the story of Romans 7 again—the war between the flesh and the spirit.

We have been stamped with the Lord's mark of ownership, the precious Holy Spirit. Not only is he the sign of our belonging, he provides the power to obey.

For you did not receive a spirit that makes you a slave again to fear, but you received the Spirit of sonship. And by him we cry, "Abba, Father." The Spirit himself testifies with our spirit that we are God's children (Romans 8:15-16).

That is true belonging, and why we are wired to belong.

The Sixth Seal—The Seal of Promise

Israel's son Judah married a Canaanite who bore him three children, Er, Onan and Shelah. In due time, Judah got a wife for Er, whose name was Tamar. When Er died childless, Judah gave her, as was the custom, to Onan. But Onan also died. Judah was afraid she carried a curse, so delayed giving her to Shelah. The story continues in Genesis 38:13-26:

When Tamar was told, "Your father-in-law is on his way to Timnah to shear his sheep," she took off her widow's clothes, covered herself with a veil to disguise herself, and then sat down at the entrance to Enaim, which is on the road to Timnah. For she saw that, though Shelah had now grown up, she had not been given to him as his wife.

When Judah saw her, he thought she was a prostitute, for she had covered her face. Not realizing that she was his daughter-in-law, he went over to her by the roadside and said, "Come now, let me sleep with you."

"And what will you give me to sleep with you?" she asked.

"I'll send you a young goat from my flock," he said.

"Will you give me something as a pledge until you send it?" she asked.

He said, "What pledge should I give you?"

"Your seal and its cord, and the staff in your hand," she answered.

So he gave them to her and slept with her, and she became pregnant by him. After she left, she took off her veil and put on her widow's clothes again.

Meanwhile Judah sent the young goat by his friend [Hiram] the Adullamite in order to get his pledge back from the woman, but he did not find her.

He asked the men who lived there, "Where is the shrine prostitute who was beside the road at Enaim?"

"There hasn't been any shrine prostitute here," they said.

So he went back to Judah and said, "I didn't find her. Besides, the men who lived there said, 'There hasn't been any shrine prostitute here.'"

Then Judah said, "Let her keep what she has, or we will become a laughingstock. After all, I did send her this young goat, but you didn't find her."

About three months later Judah was told, "Your daughter-in-law Tamar is guilty of prostitution, and as a result she is now pregnant."

Judah said, "Bring her out and have her burned to death!"

As she was being brought out, she sent a message to her father-in-law. "I am pregnant by the man who owns these," she said. And she added, "See if you recognise whose seal and cord and staff these are."

Judah recognised them and said, "She is more righteous than I, since I wouldn't give her to my son Shelah." And he did not sleep with her again.

Sheep shearing was a time of celebration which descended into drunkenness and immorality. Tamar had waited for this moment. She was bold to ask for his seal, and must have been surprised Judah was willing to give it to her. After all, it was his signature. She had to be very attractive.

But in our culture the story is bizarre. How could Judah call her prostitution "righteous"? In those days, maintaining the family line was foundational—more righteous even than acting the prostitute.

Of course she didn't want a goat, she wanted a son, whatever it took. God honoured her commitment, despite her methods, by giving her a double portion—she had twins! One even went on to be the forefather of King David and of our Messiah himself. Tamar just wanted to get pregnant. She couldn't have imagined how important her actions would be. How gracious is our God!

The story reveals the power and manner of a pledge, something given as a promise of something greater to come. The pledge is not the promise, it's merely the shadow. And so is the baptism with the Holy Spirit.

Ephesians 1:13-14 again: *Having believed, you were marked in him with a seal, the promised Holy Spirit, who is <u>a deposit guaranteeing our inheritance</u> until the redemption of those who are God's possession—to the praise of his glory.*

Our inheritance is Christ, and we are heirs of all that is his. We will live with him. We will reign with him. The wolf and the lamb will feed together and the lion will eat straw like the ox.

But we live in the already-not-yet of the in-between age. The Lord has already come and defeated the enemy on the cross. But he will return again in glory to complete his ultimate purpose. Meanwhile, the whole of creation groans in anticipation of that Day, the return of the King, and our bridegroom. This is the promise the pledge guarantees.

Engaged to Christ

When a couple become engaged, the man usually places a ring on the third finger of his fiancée's left hand. The ring symbolises the relationship, and whenever the girl gazes at it, she is reminded that her situation has changed. She is no longer a single girl, but promised.

Of course, the first thing she does is show her friends. "I am engaged. I am to be married!" And because she's in love, she will speak of him and to him for hours.

The ring has other implications. Before I came to Christ, I lived for two things—cars and girls. At parties I scanned the room for potential prospects. When I saw an attractive girl I glanced at her left hand. If I saw a ring, I hastily moved on. But no ring? Available! And I moved in.

The baptism with the Holy Spirit is our engagement ring. We

can speak in tongues, rejoicing that we're in a relationship. We can share our joy with our friends as we worship the Lord together. But the baptism is also a warning to the devil and his demons. Keep away, I am taken.

But two thousand years has been a long wait, and stretches our patience. Our longsuffering has suffered long. So we thank the Lord for this eternal guarantee. Not a one-year or even a five-year warranty, but forever, for as long as it takes. We are filled with the Spirit, and will be until the Lord takes us home or returns.

> When we stand before Christ, we can produce his seal. Marked!

When Tamar was brought out to die, she produced Judah's seal which saved her life. We shall all stand before the judgement seat of Christ, and we can produce our seal—no, <u>his</u> seal—the baptism with the Holy Spirit, to prove we belong to him. We are promised. We can wave our engagement ring and say, "Come, Lord Jesus!"

Twice fruitful

The parallels with the story of Joseph are fascinating. Remember Pharaoh had changed Joseph's name to Zaphenath-Paneah. That same verse (Genesis 41:45) continues, *and [Pharaoh] gave him Asenath daughter of Potiphera, priest of On, to be his wife.* Asenath means worshipper of Neith, an Egyptian goddess of several things, but also of creation!

But what has this to do with the seal of promise?

It amazes me that so many of Israel's descendants have foreign blood. Moses' kids were half Midianite. David's great-grandmother was the Moabitess, Ruth. It makes a mockery of anti-Semitism, in fact of all forms of racism. We are all hybrids.

Joseph's sons, Manasseh and Ephraim, were half Egyptian. Not only that, their mother worshiped idols and their grandfather was a priest of Ra, the sun god. And yet hear the Lord's heart: *"Is not Ephraim my dear son, the child in whom I delight? Though I often speak against him, I still remember him. Therefore my heart yearns for him; I have great compassion for him,"* declares the LORD (Jeremiah 31:20).

In many passages of scripture, the name Ephraim (meaning "twice fruitful") is used as a symbol or alternative for the nation of Israel. Joseph named his second son Ephraim, saying, *"It is because God has made me fruitful in the land of my suffering"* (Genesis 41:52). Like Abraham and like Jacob, Joseph named him for his future, not his past—a pledge of the Lord's promise, not only to Joseph, but to the whole nation of Israel.

And not only to Israel, but to the whole world, *"for out of Egypt I called my Son"* (Matthew 2:15), our Messiah, the Lord Jesus. Twice fruitful out of suffering. What a pledge. What a promise!

Hope

We are prepared to go through the hard yards for the rewards dangled in the distance. They say it takes ten thousand hours to become an expert. It took me four years of hard graft to get my university degree. Others have pushed through much tougher challenges.

Let us fix our eyes on Jesus, the author and perfecter of our faith, who for the joy set before him endured the cross, scorning its shame, and sat down at the right hand of the throne of God (Hebrews 12:2).

Jesus could endure the cross because of the rewards: you and I with him in the coming kingdom. We were worth it. Before the creation of the world he knew we would sin, but he came anyway. There was no greater suffering, and therefore there could be no greater reward.

It's why Abram obeyed the Lord and left his country. It's why

Moses led Israel forty years through the desert. It's why the prophets endured persecution; why Stephen was willing to be stoned; why Paul and Silas praised God in prison.

It's easy to press forward when the road is level and clear. But when we struggle for years to obey the Lord, only to be rewarded with further years of struggle, we need hope.

My wife and I moved from England to New Zealand in 2005. The other day, feeling unsettled, I caught myself speaking of England as home. But how long must I live here before this becomes home? If we returned to England, would I call New Zealand, home?

Of course, as a child of the kingdom, the answer is neither. Heaven is my home. And until we are with the Lord, our spirits will remain unsettled. Thank the Lord for the pledge of the baptism with the Holy Spirit—the divine guarantee of our eternal home-coming.

The six seals of the Holy Spirit are essential for our strength, courage, patience, long-suffering and hope. But the greatest of all is the seventh seal. The ring.

Chapter 7

The Seal of Authority

The story of Joseph and Pharaoh is about the transfer of authority. *Pharaoh said to Joseph, "I hereby put you in charge of the whole land of Egypt." Then Pharaoh took his signet ring from his finger and put it on Joseph's finger* (Genesis 41:41-42a).

We have seen the importance of the robes, the chain, the chariot, the new name and new wife! But the ring is the most important because it's the most powerful. The implications for the baptism with the Holy Spirit are huge.

Signet rings appear many times in scripture. As we have seen, in an age when few people could read or write, they were the equivalent of a person's signature, and the seal could be applied to any document to verify its authenticity—signed and sealed!

In the case of royalty, the ring could be removed and passed to anyone under the king's authority to sign his decrees. This would have been a normal process for administering the kingdom. But of course it could be misused.

In 1 Kings 21, Ahab king of Israel became grumpy because a certain Naboth refused to sell him his vineyard. Ahab's wife, Jezebel, was incensed. True to character, she hatched a plot and *wrote letters in Ahab's name, placed his seal on them,* [presumably having "borrowed" it], *and sent them to the elders and nobles who lived in Naboth's city with him* (1 Kings 21:8), inviting Naboth to a feast where he would be falsely accused and executed.

In Esther, the misuse is far more serious, threatening the whole

Israelite nation. King Xerxes had elevated Haman the Agagite (Agag was the king of the Amalekites) to the highest post in Babylon. Haman hated the Jews, and plotted their genocide. Now King Saul had failed to obey the Lord's command to totally destroy the Amalekites—it was the reason he lost the throne. The Lord knew the danger they would be to his people in the future.

But Haman had wormed his way into Xerxes' favour and even sold the king his deadly scheme. *So the king took his signet ring from his finger and gave it to Haman son of Hammedatha, the Agagite, the enemy of the Jews* (Esther 3:10). And of course with the king's signature, Haman was free to act as he wished.

In one of the most compelling stories in the Bible (I always have to read Esther in one sitting), the tables are turned. Haman is hanged on the gallows he made for his arch-enemy, Mordecai, while Esther and Mordecai are restored. Then *the king took off his signet ring, which he had reclaimed from Haman, and presented it to Mordecai. And Esther appointed him over Haman's estate* (Esther 8:2).

There follows one of the most astonishing revelations of authority in the whole of scripture, which we'll return to shortly. But first, how does all this relate to the Holy Spirit?

Zerubbabel

We have established that the baptism with the Holy Spirit is the Lord's seal of our salvation. *Having believed, you were marked in him with a seal, the promised Holy Spirit* (Ephesians 1:13b). If the Spirit is the Lord's seal, he is also the Lord's signature.

Now at the end of the book of Haggai we read this: *"'On that day,' declares the LORD Almighty, 'I will take you, my servant Zerubbabel son of Shealtiel,' declares the LORD, 'and I will make you like my signet ring, for I have chosen you,' declares the LORD Almighty"* (Haggai 2:23). "Declares the Lord" appears three times. This is important.

Of the royal line of David, Zerubbabel was the appointed governor of Jerusalem after the exile. The Lord appears to be saying he will make him like his own signature! If that is so, Zerubbabel could do whatever he felt prompted to do, knowing that the Lord will sign it off! This appears to be astonishing authority. So what does it mean?

Let's try to unwrap it. First of all the words "servant", "that day" and "chosen" can refer to the coming Messiah. Jesus would indeed become like the Lord's signature, his life a perfect reflection of his Father, the image of the invisible God. *"Any who has seen me has seen the Father,"* he said to Philip.

But it goes further. For Jesus himself passed his own authority to the church. In the Great Commission in Matthew 28, he says, *"All authority has been given to me,"* that is, he has the signature of God. Then he says, *"Therefore go!"* The command transfers the authority.

We see it again in Matthew 16. Jesus said to Peter, representing the church, *"I will give you the keys of the kingdom of heaven; whatever you bind on earth will be bound in heaven, and whatever you loose on earth will be loosed in heaven"* (Matthew 16:19). Whatever binding and loosing mean, this passes great authority to us, the church. I explain this in much greater detail in my book, *Authority* (see Recommended Reading).

We are told this will happen "on that day"! This could mean when the Messiah first comes or when the Lord returns. Or could it mean something else? For I find it intriguing that God promises to make Zerubbabel like his signet ring. Why him and not David or Moses or Elijah? Or even Joshua son of Jehozadak, the high priest, a contemporary of Zerubbabel, when the Messianic reference would be obvious because of the name and the priesthood?

Perhaps there's a clue in the name.

According to some commentators Zerubbabel means "seed of Babylon". Strong's Concordance (#2216) suggests "from Babylon" meaning he was born there or appointed from there. But the Hebrew is not at all clear. The name could even be Aramaic or Babylonian.

The Babel part is clear enough – it refers to Babylon, where he had grown up in exile. Now Babylon was the former Babel, where the people began to build a tower to reach the sky in order to make a name for themselves (see Genesis 11). So the Lord came down and confused them by making them speak different languages. Hold that thought.

The first part of Zerubbabel's name is more difficult. It could be derived from the Aramaic, *zeru*, which means seed. But equally it could derive from the Hebrew word, *zur*. (Remember Hebrew was written without vowels.)

Now according to Abarim Publications online, the verb *zur* is also used to indicate "strange" incense (as in Exodus 30:9) or "strange" fire (Leviticus 10:1).

Putting the two together, we have "strange" and "languages"! Now I am not going to build a theology on an admittedly obscure interpretation of one name. That the baptism with the Spirit is God's signature is clear enough from elsewhere. But could it be that this strange reference in Haggai refers to the baptism with the Holy Spirit, and speaking in tongues?

If so, then the prophecy refers not only to the Messiah, but also to his church. For we too are his servants, we too are chosen, and we too are baptised with the Holy Spirit, the signature of God. And if this is so, then *that day* is speaking of Pentecost, and the baptism with the Holy Spirit is the Lord's signature. What are the implications?

Astonishing authority

We return to the story of Esther. The evil Haman had been hanged. King Xerxes had given his signet ring to Mordecai, the Jew. However, Haman had passed a law that all the Jews would be killed on the thirteenth day of the twelfth month, the month of Adar. Since the laws of the Medes and Persians could never be revoked, another law had to be passed, enabling the Jews to defend themselves on that day.

Then the king said to Esther, *"Now write another decree in the king's name in behalf of the Jews as seems best to you, and seal it with the king's signet ring—for no document written in the king's name and sealed with his ring can be revoked"* (Esther 8:8).

Picture the scene. Mordecai and Esther have the king's ring. They could write what they liked, just as Haman had done, *as seems best to you*. What astonishing freedom! It is hard to comprehend, but we see the same with Pharaoh and Joseph. And what did Pharaoh say to him? *"You shall be in charge of my palace, and all my people are to submit to your orders. <u>Only with respect to the throne will I be greater than you</u>"* (Genesis 41:40).

If the baptism with the Holy Spirit is God's signature, then these phrases must also apply to us, the church. No document written in the King's name (i.e. the Bible) and sealed with his ring (the baptism with the Spirit) can be revoked. We have the King's ring. And only with respect to the throne of grace is Jesus greater than his bride. *And God raised us up with Christ and seated us with him in the heavenly realms in Christ Jesus… and if we endure, we will also reign with him.* (see Ephesians 2:6 and 2 Timothy 2:12).

> No document written in the King's name (the Bible) and sealed with his ring (the Spirit) can be revoked

I am certain the church doesn't appreciate the authority she has been given. And if we don't understand or believe it, how can we exercise it? If I give you the keys to the latest Mercedes but don't tell you, you continue to drive your old rust-bucket. Jesus has given us the keys of the kingdom of God to enable us to fulfil the Great Commission. "Therefore go!"

Chutzpah

We've discovered that each of the seven seals of the Holy Spirit have a purpose. The purpose of the seal of righteousness is faith; of proof, encouragement; of approval, assurance; of ownership, obedience; of security, perseverance; and of promise, hope.

But the purpose of the seal of authority is *chutzpah*! We have no English word that is so descriptive or so full of meaning.

"Teach us to pray," the disciples said, in Luke 11. After giving them the Lord's prayer, Jesus said, *"Suppose one of you has a friend, and he goes to him at midnight and says, 'Friend, lend me three loaves of bread.'"* In the parable, the friend refuses because the family have gone to bed. Jesus continues, *"I tell you, though he will not get up and give him the bread because he is his friend, yet because of the man's <u>boldness</u> he will get up and give him as much as he needs"* (Luke 11:8).

The NIV footnote gives persistence as an alternative to boldness. The Greek word is *anaideian*. It can be translated 'importunity' or 'impudence'. We're getting closer.

In Luke 18, Jesus told the parable of the unjust judge, commending the widow for her perseverance/importunity/cheek/guts. All these and more. The judge could have jailed her for contempt. Implied in her attitude is 1) a certainly of the justice of her cause, 2) a faith that the judge, however unjust, will eventually give in, 3) a lack of concern for her own comfort and safety. In other words, she had *chutzpah*.

How much more, then, should these be our attitudes towards the gospel and the kingdom of God? We have the Lord's signature. If we seal the Lord's word with his Spirit, it <u>must</u> come to pass. We are his ambassadors on this earth.

The baptism with the Holy Spirit is given to us to use. As we will see in the next chapters, God has given us wonderful gifts given to extend his kingdom and transform lives.

But his secret weapon is the baptism and its seven seals. We have one further seal to check out before we look at some key gifts. John, I thought you said there were seven? True. This one is a little different.

> God's secret weapon is the baptism with the Holy Spirit and the seven seals

The seal of love

The Song of Songs is a romantic musical between a lover and her beloved—a shadow of the Lord's love for his church. In chapter 8 verse 6, the beloved sings her response. *"Place me like a seal over your heart, like a seal on your arm; for love is as strong as death, its jealousy unyielding as the grave. It burns like blazing fire, like a mighty flame."*

Elijah called down fire on the soldiers in 2 Kings 1 and they died. James and John were ready to do the same to the Samaritan village who refused them bed and breakfast. Jesus rebuked them. *"Ye know not what manner of spirit ye are of. For the Son of man is not come to destroy men's lives, but to save them." And they went to another village* (Luke 9:55-56 KJV). Jesus was well aware of the effects of the fire of God. He came to offer a solution.

This new manifestation of the Holy Spirit changes everything. For the fire of love is greater still. Like the law of Mordecai and

Esther, it supersedes the law of Haman. Like the law of life in Christ Jesus, it supersedes the law of sin and death (see Romans 8:1).

In the parable of the Song of Songs, we are the beloved, so this seal is ours, not his. Therefore it is not his gift to us; it is our response to his beauty and grace. *Place me like a seal over your heart, like a seal on your arm.* The heart represents our love for Jesus, the arm our willingness to act. It is his heart (his compassion) and his arm (his strength), but we ask to be placed there. Who has not prayed, "Lord give me your strength"? Who has not prayed, "Lord, I need your compassion"?

> *Place me like a seal over your heart, like a seal on your arm*
> (Songs 8:6)

The kingdom of God cannot be extended by words alone. This book is meaningless unless we respond to the Spirit's prompting. Are we willing to act? If we are the seal over his heart, we will.

The baptism with the Holy Spirit is the Lord's signet ring. Astonishingly, he has passed it to the church. We have his authority to extend the kingdom of God by fulfilling his commands—preach the gospel, heal the sick, cast out demons, raise the dead, making disciples of all nations. When we decree the word of the Lord by the power of the Spirit, what we bind on earth will be bound in heaven. Let us be full of the *chutzpah* we will need to do it!

~ ✚ ~

Jesus promised, *"But you will receive power when the Holy Spirit comes on you; and you will be my witnesses in Jerusalem, and in all Judea and Samaria, and to the ends of the earth"* (Acts 1:8). But what does this look like in practice? How do we make it work in our daily lives?

When the twelve Ephesian brothers were baptised with the Holy Spirit in Acts 19, we read, *When Paul placed his hands on them, the Holy Spirit came on them, and they spoke in tongues and prophesied* (Acts 19:6).

Speaking in tongues and prophesying are the two main signs that we have been filled with the Spirit. Both are important, but many churches are wary of the gifts of the Spirit, as they are open to abuse. Understandably, pastors are reticent to deal with the consequent issues. They have enough on their plate as it is.

This is a pity. The Lord gave us his gifts because we need them. And from what I have experienced in many churches around the world, the problems are largely due to the fact that we aren't exercising the gifts in the ways advised by scripture. Let us therefore take another look at the gifts of the Spirit, and especially tongues and prophecy.

How can we use these safely and still be effective?

Chapter 8

Should we use Tongues in Church?

Many have written excellent books on these things, but I need to share what the Lord has put on my heart. For like the power tools in my workshop, the manifestations of the Spirit are wonderful when used properly and safely. But like them, they can be dangerous.

What are they?

Now to each one the manifestation of the Spirit is given for the common good. To one there is given through the Spirit <u>the message of wisdom</u>, to another th<u>e message of knowledge</u> by means of the same Spirit, to another <u>faith</u> by the same Spirit, to another <u>gifts of healing</u> by that one Spirit, to another <u>miraculous powers</u>, to another <u>prophecy</u>, to another <u>distinguishing between spirits</u>, to another <u>speaking in different kinds of tongues</u>, and to still another <u>the interpretation of tongues</u>. All these are the work of one and the same Spirit, and he gives them to each one, just as he determines (1 Corinthians 12:7-11).

The clear purpose is to build up the church. They are *given for the common good*. They are God's idea, not ours. If he thinks we need them, we need them. Worse, if we doubt, or ignore, or refuse, or even over-regulate the gifts, we are actually hindering the extension of the kingdom of God in the way he intended. Just as a plant needs water, the church needs them to grow.

We are baptised with the Holy Spirit. We have the Lord's signature. As the Lord's ambassadors, we have a duty to use his power to extend his kingdom. We cannot do it alone. So the Spirit gives us his gifts, the Lord's power-tools. In John chapter four, it was a word of knowledge that turned the conversation with the woman of Sychar.

One night at a Bible week some years ago, the preacher said there were three people in the tent involved in homosexual relationships, and the Lord wanted to set them free. One was a woman. He then described the contents of her handbag in astonishing detail, down to the monogram on her handkerchief. He invited them to talk to him afterwards.

The next night he said all three had repented and been delivered. I never forgot those words of knowledge. Only the Lord and the individual could know. Since then we've seen hundreds healed and set free through the use of such words.

Outside an English supermarket one afternoon, we approached three young teens to share the gospel. They mocked and giggled. In my head I heard the word "singer", so I asked the older girl if that was true.

She looked shocked and said, "Are you psychic or something?"

"No," I said, "that was the Holy Spirit." We then shared the gospel and led her to Christ. I'll say it again because it's important—if we are not using these gifts in our churches and in our lives, his kingdom will not grow as God wants.

Why Tongues?

The Holy Spirit: an Introduction by John Bevere is one of the best books on the Spirit in recent years, and with his kind permission I have drawn some of this understanding from there.

I was preaching recently in a church where tongues had been used quite freely during the service. Afterwards a man approached me. "I thought we weren't supposed to speak in tongues in church." He quoted several scriptures by heart; he obviously knew his Bible! However, there are many references to tongues in the New Testament, many of which appear to contradict each other. So this Bible man is excused for being puzzled.

We've already seen that tongues is a bizarre manifestation of the Spirit. What was God thinking of? Why should we speak in a language we don't understand? Here are four reasons:

It's personal between you and God

Tongues is our kingdom language! *If you praise him in the private language of tongues, God understands you but <u>no one else does</u>, for you are sharing intimacies just between you and him* (1 Corinthians 14:2 MSG).

> Our private conversation with God in tongues is encrypted

Our private spiritual language is not only a hotline to the Father, it's encrypted! What's more, if no one else understands, neither does the devil. How frustrated he must be when we pray or praise God in tongues and cut the enemy out of the conversation.

It's therefore useful in deliverance ministry, when we're seeking the Spirit's discernment and guidance. Demons are uncomfortable with tongues, and may leave more readily. Similarly, tongues can change the atmosphere in a building or meeting.

It builds our spirit

But you, dear friends, build yourselves up in your most holy faith and pray in the Holy Spirit (Jude 1:20). Praying in the Spirit means praying in tongues. He is the one who generates the language, not us. The language part of our brain is inactive. (The motor part is busy with our mouth and voice.) *For if I pray in a tongue, my spirit prays, but my mind is unfruitful* (1 Corinthians 14:14).

Speaking in tongues strengthens our own spirit, because it is Spirit to spirit. *He who speaks in a tongue edifies himself* (1 Corinthians 14:4a). It bypasses the world, the flesh and the devil. No logic, no distractions, no negative words, no human desires or ambition can distract our communication with the Lord.

We can pray beyond our understanding

In the same way, the Spirit helps us in our weakness. We do not know what we ought to pray for, but the Spirit himself intercedes for us with groans that words cannot express. And he who searches our hearts knows the mind of the Spirit, because the Spirit intercedes for the saints in accordance with God's will (Romans 8:26-27).

The Spirit's words are creative. We may not know what we pray, but we can be sure it is what the Lord wants and will achieve his purpose. It's impossible to know all that the Lord would have us pray about—his ways are above our ways. Not to worry; we can intercede in tongues, as we will see.

It requires submission

To allow the Spirit to use our body, especially for something we don't understand, is an act of both surrender and trust. This humility honours God and opens the door for him to be able to use us in other gifts. That's why it is usually the first sign of the baptism with the Holy Spirit.

It truly is out of our mind: *So if the whole church comes together and everyone speaks in tongues, and some who do not understand or some unbelievers come in, will they not say that you are out of your mind?* (1 Corinthians 14:23)—out of our mind, yes, but into our spirit. It is a conscious decision to yield to the Spirit, allowing him to do with us as he wills.

The Four Types of Tongues

It helped me unravel some of the puzzle (there are still puzzles) to understand there are various kinds of tongues, used for different purposes. 1 Corinthians 12:10 refers to *different kinds of tongues*, and 1 Corinthians 13:1 gives another clue: *If I speak in the tongues of men and of angels, but have not love, I am only a resounding gong or a clanging cymbal.*

So speaking in the Spirit can result in tongues of both men (languages someone in the world will understand), and angels (which, presumably, no one understands.) At Pentecost everyone heard the disciples praising God in their own languages. Tongues of men. But then there's our encrypted hotline to the Father. Tongues of angels. Different kinds.

In fact there seem to be four types of tongues – two for private use, and two for public use. The confusion comes because they are intended for different purposes and different places. We therefore need to understand which scriptures apply to which kind. In fact, some scriptures refer to more than one kind in a couple of verses. It confused me for many years, and I trust this will bring some clarity to those like our confused Bible man.

So what are the four kinds?

Private, for personal use

This is our personal communication with the Lord. We've already quoted 1 Corinthians 14:2, where we are *sharing intimacies just between you and him*. We can burble away in tongues daily or even hourly.

1 Corinthians 14:13-17 tells us we can also praise God and give thanks both in our mind and in our spirit, speaking or singing. We are connecting with God, our spirits uploading and downloading heavenly messages.

I have found I can even pray in tongues under my breath—the Spirit language rolling around in my spirit—especially wonderful at night or in awkward situations where speaking aloud might bring offense.

Secondly, as we've seen, speaking in tongues edifies our spirit. The Apostle Paul said, *"I thank God that I speak in tongues more than all of you"* (1 Corinthians 14:18). On missions trips we spend many hours travelling. I use these times to pray in tongues, so when we come to the meetings, my spirit is ready. I pray in tongues more than I do with words.

This is tongues for private use, when I am not communicating with anyone except the Lord.

Private, for intercession

> Praying in the Spirit is taking the battle to the enemy

A friend woke late one night compelled to pray without knowing why. So she prayed in tongues for some time, and found herself repeating an unfamiliar word. The next day she heard the news that a town of that name had suffered an earthquake. She'd been praying for them totally unaware.

We do not know what we ought to pray for, but the Spirit himself intercedes for us. How many lives were saved through her intercession we cannot know, but we can be sure it helped.

In the passage in Ephesians 6 about spiritual warfare, Paul writes, *For our struggle is not against flesh and blood, but against the rulers, against the authorities, against the powers of this dark world and against the spiritual forces of evil in the heavenly realms* (Ephesians 6:12). He then instructs us to put on the whole armour of God, ending with this: *And pray in the Spirit on all occasions with all kinds of prayers and requests. With this in mind, be alert and always keep on praying for all the saints* (Ephesians 6:18). Praying in the Spirit is taking the battle to the enemy.

We were ministering to a girl with demons, which were reluctant to come out. I felt a prompting in my spirit to speak over her in tongues. She manifested violently, and finally the demons left.

Another time we were invited to the home of a new believer. She said it had an atmosphere and thought it haunted. We marched around the house praying in tongues and anointing the doors and walls with oil.

We descended to the cellar. It was freezing! Aware that can be a sign of witchcraft, we repeated our intercession, anointing the whole cellar with oil. The new believer told us the house was no longer haunted and the cellar was warm. We later discovered the cellar had indeed been used for witchcraft.

We have the gift of tongues to help us fight the good fight. We have no idea how powerful this gift is in the spirit realm. But if the Lord gave it to us to use, then let's use it.

These are the two types of tongues for private use—for personal edification and praise, and for intercession.

There are also two types for use in public:

Tongues for a sign

When the Lord poured out his Spirit at Pentecost, he wanted the world to know. The disciples began speaking in at least fifteen different languages known to man. As intended this drew a crowd,

Peter preached the best sermon of his life, and *three thousand were added to their number that day.*

In Poland, a friend was praying for a line of people. He felt to pray over one man in tongues. Immediately the man took a pack of cigarettes from his pocket and threw it to the floor. Thinking the Spirit had convicted the man, my friend smiled and moved down the line. He later returned to the man, and again prayed over him in tongues. The man stamped on the pack, crushing them with his foot.

My friend's interpreter was astonished. "You told me you speak no Polish and you need an interpreter for everything. But now you've spoken twice to this man in perfect Polish!"

"What did I say?"

"First you told him to throw his cigarettes away. Then you told him to destroy them."

John Bevere tell this story:

> Several years ago I was preaching at a church in Colorado Springs. During the service one of my staff members was sitting in the back of the church. The whole time I was preaching, she felt the urge to quietly pray in tongues. When the service was over, a gentleman who was sitting in front of her approached her and said, "Your French is perfect. You even speak with a perfect accent of the ancient French dialect. I'm a French teacher, and in all my years, I've never encountered someone who speaks French as well as you do."
>
> My staff member responded, "I don't speak French." The man was shocked.
>
> He said, "Not only were you speaking perfect French, but you were also quoting scriptures in French. Then John would have the congregation turn to those same scriptures. You quoted them before he even said them." (John P. Bevere, Jr. *The*

Holy Spirit: An introduction, p. 129).

When people are speaking in a language they do not know, it has to be God. It's a sign, usually to unbelievers, that God is real and that he cares. Even though they had no idea what they were saying, the disciples at Pentecost *were declaring the wonders of God*, not berating the crowd. This unique sign produced plenty of fruit that day.

Tongues for interpretation

I first heard tongues interpreted on a missions' trip. As we were leaving a pastor's home, one of our team began speaking in tongues. But the tone was different from our earlier prayers—more forceful. It carried weight. One of our team then gave the interpretation, a prophetic encouragement for the pastor.

1 Corinthians 12:10 refers to the interpretation of tongues as one of the nine manifestations of the Spirit mentioned in that passage. Some believe interpretation is focused on the wonders of the Lord, that is, praise *toward* God, rather than a prophetic message *from* him. However, I have witnessed interpretation used for both reasons, and the Spirit was clearly involved.

When the Spirit is flowing in a meeting, tongues and interpretation can move almost instantly from person to person. However, this shouldn't be chaotic: *If anyone speaks in a tongue, two—or at the most three—should speak, one at a time, and someone must interpret* (1 Corinthians 14:27). In the church meetings in Corinth, everyone had been speaking loudly to each other in tongues. Paul rebuked them, saying, *Brothers, stop thinking like children. In regard to evil be infants, but in your thinking be adults* (1 Corinthians 14:20). Unless it's interpreted, that is pointless. Actually, it's worse, as we'll see.

So the usual order is tongue, interpretation, tongue, interpretation. But the Bible also allows for tongue, tongue, tongue, interpretations.

In such a meeting I find the Spirit bubbles up within me with an urgency to speak more forcibly, which is different from the normal use of tongues. Similarly, we recognise a tongue that requires interpretation in the same way. One message in tongues can receive several interpretations, sometimes quite different. Similarly, several different tongues can receive a very similar interpretation.

We've even witnessed a "tongue" being given through music. In a meeting in Jamaica, the band was jamming when suddenly the drums took on a different timbre—again, more weighty. The drummer continued for about one minute. Everyone felt the anointing of the Spirit, and when he stopped the church fell silent. Then a member of the congregation brought the interpretation, a powerful prophetic message for the church.

These are the four types of tongues we meet in the scriptures: privately for personal use and for intercession; and publicly as a sign to unbelievers and for interpretation.

But that returns to our question. Should we use tongues in church, and if so, how and when? First, we need to make sense of two passages in 1 Corinthians which seem to be contradictory.

Making Sense of 1 Corinthians 12:30

In chapter 12, Paul lists the gifts we've addressed above. The chapter concludes: *27Now you are the body of Christ, and each one of you is a part of it.*

28And in the church God has appointed [notice, these are appointments] *first of all apostles, second prophets, third teachers, then workers of miracles, also those having gifts of healing, those able to help others, those with gifts of administration, and those speaking in different kinds of tongues.*

²⁹*Are all apostles? Are all prophets? Are all teachers? Do all work miracles? Do all have gifts of healing? Do all speak in tongues? Do all interpret? But eagerly desire the greater gifts* (1 Corinthians 12:27-31a).

We are all different, with different gifts to bring to the table. But the questions clearly imply not everyone has all the gifts. However, that raises a problem.

When we receive the Spirit, as I've already said, he comes as a Person, not a thing. Therefore we cannot have a little bit of the Spirit—we either have him with us or we don't. And if he's with us, all his gifts must be available to us. In 1 Corinthians 12:11 we read, a*ll these are the work of one and the same Spirit, and he gives them to each one, just as he determines.*

> The gifts of the Spirit are the toolbox of the kingdom of God

Now, that last phrase can be interpreted in two ways: just as the Spirit determines, or just as each one determines. I am no Greek scholar, but apparently the syntax prefers the latter. If that is so, then all the gifts are the toolbox of the kingdom of God, available to everyone filled with the Spirit to use as appropriate for each situation, whether at the prompting of the Spirit or the decision of the person.

In which case, there's a contradiction with the passage at the end of the chapter. Can we all use all the gifts, or only the one or two given to each of us?

Because we have the Spirit, I believe all of us can access all of the Spirit's gifts when the need arises. By God's grace, I have used them all myself. However, I do not consider myself to be an apostle or a miracle worker, although I have seen amazing miracles through our ministry.

I believe we have the authority to step out in faith to apply the gifts as and when we feel appropriate. (And that feeling is guided by the Spirit anyway.) After all, if we are sensitive to the Spirit, we will want what he wants and wish to help those he wishes to help. That's what the gifts are for.

But I also believe that some have special gifts or callings or appointments. I am a teacher. My wife has a gift of healing frozen shoulders—probably about 90 percent of those she ministers to receive healing. Only two days ago a man was healed, waving his arm in the air saying, "I can't do that." Praise God!

Paul concludes 1 Corinthians 12 with *do all speak in tongues?* The implication is that not everyone who is baptised with the Holy Spirit can and does speak in tongues. However, when people were baptised with the Spirit in the book of Acts, mostly they did. It seemed to be the main sign of the baptism. So what's going on?

Now we understand the four types of tongues, we find Paul refers to the different types in different scriptures without identifying which type he is meaning. So in order to make sense of Paul's question in 1 Corinthians 12:30, we must try to identify the type he is referring to.

All the gifts mentioned throughout 1 Corinthians 12 are *given for the common good*, that is, <u>for public use</u>. Therefore, in 1 Corinthians 12:30 he is still referring to public ministry, that is, tongues for interpretation or tongues for a sign. Hold that thought.

Now in 1 Corinthians 14 he switches focus, dealing with the relative importance of tongues <u>for private use</u> and prophecy. What does he say? *I would like every one of you to speak in tongues* (verse 5). Why? *For anyone who speaks in a tongue does not speak to men but to God. Indeed, no one understands him; he utters mysteries with his spirit* (1 Corinthians 14:2), and, *he who speaks in a tongue edifies himself* (1

Corinthians 14:4a). So these are clearly for private, not public use.

The main point Paul is making in that chapter is speaking in tongues for private use when we are together is pretty pointless if we are trying to communicate with each other. No one will understand, *unless he interprets so that the church may be edified.* (Note the purpose of interpretation—the building up or encouragement of the church.)

He goes on to say, *I thank God that I speak in tongues* [tongues for private use] *more than all of you. But in the church I would rather speak five intelligible words to instruct others than ten thousand words in a* [private use] *tongue* (1 Corinthians 14:18-19).

So coming back to the question in 1 Corinthians 12:30, *do all speak in tongues?* The answer is no, if it's for public use, but, hopefully yes, if it's for private use.

Some are baptised with the Holy Spirit, but don't yet speak in tongues. I believe all who have been baptised with the Holy Spirit have his gifts available to them, including tongues. If you are in this situation, be encouraged. You have the Spirit, so step out in faith, and exercise the gifts he has given you, by faith.

We now come to further apparent confusion.

Making sense of 1 Corinthians 14:22-25

At the end of the complicated passage on tongues and prophecy, we find this summary:

²²*Tongues, then, are a sign, not for believers but for unbelievers; prophecy, however, is for believers, not for unbelievers.*

²³*So if the whole church comes together and everyone speaks in tongues, and some who do not understand or some unbelievers come in, will they not say that you are out of your mind?*

²⁴*But if an unbeliever or someone who does not understand comes in while everybody is prophesying, he will be convinced by all that he is a*

sinner and will be judged by all, ²⁵and the secrets of his heart will be laid bare. So he will fall down and worship God, exclaiming, "God is really among you!" (1 Corinthians 14:22-25).

In these four verses, Paul appears to contradict himself, twice. First, he says tongues are a sign for unbelievers, but then says if unbelievers come in when everyone is speaking in tongues, they'll say you're out of your mind. So is it a sign, or isn't it?

Next, he says that prophecy is for believers, not for unbelievers. But he goes on to say if everyone is prophesying, unbelievers will be convinced they are sinners and worship God. So who is it for, believers or unbelievers?

Looking at the second issue first, when Paul says prophecy is for believers, he is meaning for believers to use. Unbelievers do not have the gift of prophecy, (though they can have a spirit of divination,) because they do not have the Holy Spirit. So prophecy is for believers to use in our meetings, so that unbelievers will be convicted. More of this in the next chapter.

What about the first apparent contradiction? Soon after I had become a Christian, I began searching for a church. I was too proud to attend our own village church, so I tried traditional churches in our local town. They were as boring as I remembered. One Sunday I plucked up courage and entered a Pentecostal church. I am sure they greeted me kindly, but I sat at the back in trepidation. After the first song, everyone raised their hands in the air and spoke loudly in tongues for several minutes. I thought they were nuts and made a hasty exit.

So should we use tongues in church, or not?

I believe we can unravel these verses by realising Paul is referring to two different kinds of tongues in two verses. Let's look at 1 Corinthians 14:22-23 again, with some commentary:

Tongues, then, are a sign [tongues for a sign, i.e. for public use], *not for* [the purpose of convincing] *believers but for* [convincing] *unbelievers; prophecy, however, is for believers* [to use], *not for unbelievers* [to use, because they don't have the Spirit.]

²³*So if the whole church comes together and everyone speaks in tongues* [tongues for private use, not for public use], *and some who do not understand or some unbelievers come in, will they not say that you are out of your mind?* Just as I did!

This is why Paul emphasises that if someone brings a message in tongues, it must be interpreted. *If anyone speaks in a tongue, two—or at the most three—should speak, one at a time, and someone must interpret* (1 Corinthians 14:27). How do you know that the person behind you isn't someone like me, ready to make a hasty retreat? Let's be honest, tongues is bizarre!

Therefore using tongues in public, *when the whole church comes together*, should be for the two public use types of tongues—for a sign to convict unbelievers or for interpretation, so that the church may be edified. The use of tongues for these purposes should be encouraged in our meetings. They bring a dynamic of the Spirit we could not know otherwise. It also opens the door for other gifts, such healings, miracles and prophecy.

Will they also open the door for the weird? Yes! So it's important to have some controls in place. If you are leading, and want to introduce these gifts to your meetings, first practice the gifts yourself. Then teach the people how they work, encouraging them to step out in faith, perhaps first in home groups or church prayer meetings, where it's a safer environment.

In public meetings, set a time for the operation of the gifts, explain what is happening, and honour those who step out. At the same time, be willing to confirm words that are from the Holy Spirit. For those words you feel uncomfortable about, that cut across what the Spirit is doing, or flow against the culture of your church, be honest and courageous enough to say so, without putting the person down.

For example: "Thank you, John, for your courage and interpretation. I am not sure that is a word for the church at this time, but let's pray about it." If the same person keeps bringing such words, counsel them privately, guiding them to the right path. And if they refuse, ask them to keep silent in the church or leave.

In open church meetings, where *some who do not understand or some unbelievers* may come in, using tongues for private use (for prayer, intercession, praise or personal edification) should be discouraged, unless it's explained. We should use our gifts, sensitive to the needs of those present. If people wish to speak, sing or pray in tongues privately, they should be encouraged to do so quietly.

> If we want to use tongues for private use in public meetings, we should explain to those who don't understand

Of course in prayer meetings without unbelievers present, we are free to speak, pray and sing as we wish! But if we want to use tongues for private use in public meetings, we should explain what is happening to those who do not understand. This is just common courtesy. And it would have been kind to our Bible man who wanted to know what was going on.

In summary then, if you are leading services or meetings open to the public:

- Encourage public use of tongues for interpretation
- Encourage public use of tongues for a sign, using a known language

- Discourage praying aloud in tongues for private use, unless it's explained
- Tongues for private use should be silent or very quiet
- Train your people to know the difference

As a believer attending public meetings, follow the above pattern, being sensitive to those who may not understand.

However, much more powerful is for everyone to prophesy.

Chapter 9

Be Eager to Prophesy

I had taught a successful seven-week prophecy course at our church, teaching over one hundred to use the gift. During the training, God used them powerfully and they were excited.

The next Sunday one of our members felt prompted to share a word of prophecy with the lady behind her, a stranger. The member explained we'd been doing the course, and asked if she could share what she felt was from the Holy Spirit. The lady agreed. The word proved to be very accurate, and the recipient was totally astonished. Not only was she an unbeliever, it was her first time in church! Needless to say, she returned the next week, and surrendered her life to Christ.

But if an unbeliever or someone who does not understand comes in while everybody is prophesying, he will be convinced by all that he is a sinner and will be judged by all, and the secrets of his heart will be laid bare. So he will fall down and worship God, exclaiming, "God is really among you!" (1 Corinthians 14:24-25).

Prophecy is the most important of the gifts of the Spirit. *Follow the way of love and eagerly desire spiritual gifts, <u>especially the gift of prophecy</u>* (1 Corinthians 14:1).

If it's so important, shouldn't it have a greater place in our churches? Do you have a pastor in your church? Of course. Do you have an evangelist or two? Probably. Do you have any prophets or prophetesses?

At least a quarter of the Bible is prophecy, yet it's been

neglected in the church worldwide for centuries. However, interest is returning, and many churches are now encouraging prophecy, although it is still largely exercised by those on the platform—the pastor or visiting speakers. That isn't the picture we find in scripture.

Prophecy is simply speaking words that come from God: *If anyone speaks, he should do it as one speaking the very words of God... so that in all things God may be praised through Jesus Christ* (see 1 Peter 4:11).

The problem is no one wants to either get it wrong or be a false prophet. Actually these two are quite different.

A false prophet is sent by the enemy to disturb, disrupt and divide the church. They prophesy out of a wrong spirit or their own mind. *For prophecy never had its origin in the will of man, but men spoke from God as they were carried along by the Holy Spirit* (2 Peter 1:21).

> False prophets and false prophecy are quite different

However, everyone who prophesies will get it wrong sometimes. We must be humble enough to risk making mistakes, and gracious to accept those made by genuine learners.

To be *carried along by the Holy Spirit* means it must be initiated by God, we must act in obedience to share it, and often the Spirit then gives us more as we speak.

But how do we know it's from him?

Training

In 1 Corinthians 12:28, we read, *God has appointed first of all apostles, second prophets, third teachers*. In Ephesians 4:11, Paul tells us the Lord *gave some to be apostles, some to be prophets*. In Ephesians 2:20, it says the church is built on the foundation of the apostles and prophets.

Clearly, apostles and prophets are the most important offices in the church. But in our Bible colleges, who do we train? Pastors and teachers. Maybe some evangelists. I never heard of a prophet being trained in Bible College. Elisha trained a large company of prophets (see 2 Kings chapters 2 to 6). They were good too. They accurately prophesied the day of Elijah's departure. Even King Saul met with them and prophesied. Do we have our priorities right?

Some argue that since prophecy is a gift of the Spirit, why should we need training? Shouldn't we just flow with the Spirit? Well, in order to flow with the Spirit, we have to know the Spirit. (We'll look at that in more detail in the next chapter.)

Samuel was one of the greatest prophets in the Old Testament. None of his words fell to the ground, and yet as a boy he didn't recognise God's voice. *For the word of the Lord had not yet been revealed to him* (1 Samuel 3:7). When God called him, he ran to the high priest, Eli, thinking the voice was his. Three times he ran, until Eli realised what was going on. *So Eli told Samuel, "Go and lie down, and if he calls you, say, 'Speak, LORD, for your servant is listening.'"* (1 Samuel 3:9a). Only then did Samuel realise it was the Lord.

If Samuel had to learn to hear the voice of God, how much more do we? In our courses, we find people's greatest concerns are that God doesn't speak to them, and if he did, how would they know it was him? But once people understand, the Lord uses them powerfully.

The Lord speaks, but we need to be trained.

Why Prophesy?

We are urged to
Be eager to prophesy (1 Corinthians 14:39). Paul isn't writing to church leaders, but to every believer. *But Moses replied, "Are you jealous for my sake? I wish that all the LORD's people were prophets and that the LORD would put his Spirit on them!"* (Numbers 11:29). The Lord wants everyone to prophesy.

Prophecy builds up the church
The whole tenor of 1 Corinthians 14 is that prophecy edifies the church. *For you can all prophesy in turn so that everyone may be instructed and encouraged* (1 Corinthians 14:31).

It builds up people
But everyone who prophesies speaks to men for their strengthening, encouragement and comfort (1 Corinthians 14:3). The clear implication is that without prophecy we cannot be strengthened, encouraged or comforted in the way the Lord wants.

It convicts sinners
We have already seen its effect on unbelievers. The secrets of their hearts are laid bare.

It influences the future!
Zechariah didn't believe the angel Gabriel's prophecy. Gabriel prophesied again. *"And now you will be silent and not able to speak."* The priest became dumb.

When Paul met Elymas the sorcerer in Cyprus, he prophesied, *"You are going to be blind and for a time you will be unable to see the light of the sun." Immediately mist and darkness came over him, and he groped about, seeking someone to lead him by the hand* (Acts 13:11).

Their prophetic words had power.

The Lord actually works to fulfil his own words. *This is what the LORD says... who foils the signs of false prophets ... who carries out the words of his servants and fulfils the predictions of his messengers* (Isaiah 44:24-26). These verses strongly imply that when false prophets make predictions, the Lord makes sure it doesn't come to pass.

Equally, (and we say this humbly), when believers prophesy in his Name, then he works things out to ensure that, as long as it's consistent with his overall purpose, it does come to pass, and his Name is therefore honoured.

What prophecy is not for

If it is to encourage people and build the church, anything that doesn't do that is not God. Jesus said, *"I will build my church,"* not destroy it.

Therefore prophecy should not be used for controlling, commanding or manipulating people. Actually, that is witchcraft. The Lord will never <u>demand</u> obedience. He invites it, and may warn against the risks of disobedience, but "you must" has no place in genuine prophecy.

We do not use prophecy to condemn, judge or criticise. The devil is the accuser; the Lord is an encourager. He is a forgiver. If he does rebuke, he always offers a solution. When Jesus rebuked the Ephesian church in Revelation 2:1-7, he first of all praises them for their hard work and endurance. Then he shows them they have forsaken their first love. Then he gives the solution. *"Repent,"* he says, *"and do the things you did at first,"* promising the tree of life to those who overcome. The Spirit convicts. The devil condemns.

Prophecy is not to tell people who they will marry, when the Lord is returning or how much to put in the offering. It is not to be used for mates, dates and rates!

> Prophecy is not for mates, dates and rates!

I have heard amazing detail in prophecy, but there always remains a sense of mystery. Some prophecies are deliberately obscure. I believe the Lord wants us to pray them through, seeking clarification. At the same time, they often confirm what the Lord has been saying through prayer, the Bible, or the wise counsel of others.

How God Speaks

In the scriptures, the Lord speaks in over forty ways: from fire to thunder, from angels to donkeys. Creation, clouds, coincidence; poetry, prophecy, prophetic acts; even a still small voice—the list goes on and on. He is a creative God. He made the universe by speaking and he continues to speak. Unlike the mute idols, he's a speaking God—it's one way we recognise him.

He is our Father, and we are his kids, so it shouldn't come as a surprise that he speaks to us regularly. John 8:47 says, *"He who belongs to God hears what God says."* Do you belong to God? Then you hear him! And yet so many feel that he doesn't speak to them, or if he does, it's only rarely. Be encouraged! He *is* speaking, but like Samuel, we often don't realise it's him.

Actually, I believe he is speaking to us all the time. How?

By his Spirit

All day long I have two voices in my head, assessing, discussing and sometimes arguing. I used to be told it was a sign of madness. If so, I've discovered we are all mad, as everyone has these two voices. So what are they?

According to 1 Thessalonians 5:3, we are made of three parts—spirit, soul and body. We <u>are</u> a spirit, we <u>have</u> a soul, and we walk around in a body. Our soul is the part of us that makes us who we are. It consists of our mind, will and emotions, often referred to in scripture as our heart.

Now 1 Corinthians 2:11 says, *for who among men knows the thoughts of a man except the man's spirit within him? In the same way no one knows the thoughts of God except the Spirit of God.* Our thoughts come from our mind, and our mind is part of our soul. If our spirit knows our thoughts, then they are in constant communication. Which explains the two voices in our heads—our spirit speaking to our soul.

Paul goes on: *We have not received the spirit of the world but the Spirit who is from God, that we may understand what God has freely given us. This is what we speak, not in words taught us by human wisdom but in words taught by the Spirit, expressing spiritual truths in spiritual words* (1 Corinthians 2:12-13).

When we surrender our lives to Christ, his Spirit takes up residence in our spirit. *Do you not know that your body is a temple of the Holy Spirit, who is in you, whom you have received from God?* (1 Corinthians 6:19). The temple is a parable. It had an outer court (our body), an inner sanctum (our soul), and a holy of holies (our spirit). The former had to be purified, but the holy of holies only once a year, by the high priest, and never without blood (see Hebrews 9:6-9).

Jesus has paid once for all by his blood so that the Holy Spirit can dwell in our spirits, his holy of holies. Spiritually, we are a new creation, born of the Spirit. (Although our soul still requires a lot of sanctification.)

Therefore the new resident in our spirits is the Holy Spirit. So now the conversation in our head must be between our mind (our soul), and the Holy Spirit. This means God is speaking to believers **all the time**. That is why Paul ends this astonishing passage in scripture with the even more astonishing *but we have the mind of Christ*. How? By his (talking) Spirit, resident in ours.

> John Bevere writes:
>
> A number of years ago, I was driving when I heard the Holy Spirit say, "I have something to say. Pull off the road." Now I've learned that when God tells me to do something—even if it appears trivial or is inconvenient at the time—to obey. Instantly. A half mile down the highway I pulled off at a rest stop.
>
> Immediately, I heard the Spirit of God whisper to my heart, "Did I not say to you, 'Pray without ceasing'?"
>
> I responded, "Yes Lord, You did."
>
> He probed further. "Is prayer a monologue or a dialogue?"
>
> I replied, "It's a dialogue Lord, a two-way conversation."
>
> His words came quickly. "Well, if I said to pray without ceasing, then that means I am willing to communicate without ceasing!"
>
> It was a pivotal moment for me. I realized God wants to speak to us far more than we typically engage with Him.

> The Father speaks to his children all the time

So if God really is speaking to us all the time by his Spirit, how do we know which voice is me and which is God? And what about the devil? Doesn't he speak into our mind as well?

Recognising his voice

Jesus says, *"The man who enters by the gate is the shepherd of his sheep... and the sheep listen to his voice. He calls his own sheep by name and leads them out"* (John 10:2-3). How do they know?

We keep sheep on our few acres. When they first arrived, if we called they'd retreat to the far end of the paddock. After some weeks of feeding, they came running to our call; they have learned our voices. We come to know the voice of the Lord by familiarity.

Of course the main ways we learn his voice are in prayer and the Bible. These reveal his nature and his methods. He will never speak out of character, and never contrary to his *logos* word, the scriptures. It's important we know them.

We hear his "now" (*rhema*) word usually at first from his Spirit in our heads, although he often speaks through dreams, visions, songs, and pictures.

The still, small voice

After his colossal triumph on Mount Carmel, Elijah ran. He ran to overtake Ahab's chariot. Then he ran from Jezebel's threats. He ran for his life, the Bible says, and wanted to die. He complained to the Lord he was the only prophet left. But the Lord hadn't finished with him yet. He sent him forty days to Mount Horeb, to hear his voice, not in the rock-shattering wind, not the earthquake, not the fire. Then came the still, small voice—a "gentle whisper", my NIV calls it.

I believe the whisper was in his heart all the time, but Elijah was too preoccupied with his own zeal (pride), his own safety (fear), or his depression (hopelessness) to hear. They can hinder us too.

Jesus told the unbelievers they couldn't hear his words because they were children of the devil. His own disciples couldn't "hear" his warnings about his impending death, because of their mindset; it made no sense to them, so they dismissed it as impossible, "He couldn't mean *that*!"

But even if we can hear, we may not listen, and we can listen, but not obey! However, Jesus says, *"What I tell you in the dark, speak in the daylight; what is whispered in your ear, proclaim from the roofs"* (Matthew 10:27). We are expected to share what we are given. The gifts of the Spirit operate by faith. Like Peter stepping out of the boat, we step out as though we can, knowing we can't.

My first mission trip was a weeklong pastors' conference in Poland. I was the bus driver. A new believer, I was in awe of the great men of God on our team and I sat at the back soaking up their teaching. During worship on the third day, I felt the Lord say, "I want you to prophesy."

> Faith is stepping out as though you can, knowing you can't

I argued. "Lord, I am the bus driver. There are two hundred pastors here, plus our own team." But after five minutes, I finally gave in. "Okay, Lord, tell me what to say, and I'll go."

"No," he said, "you go, and I'll tell you what to say."

My heart thumping, I walked to the front. The girl leading suddenly stopped playing. Four hundred eyes opened. I sweated. "I have a word from the Lord," I said. It was a lie. I had nothing!

She gave me the microphone, and immediately I saw a picture of Poland like an old wineskin being filled, the new wine bursting out into neighbouring countries. When I opened my eyes, everyone was crying.

Often we must go before we have the word.

The voice of the enemy

Although the Lord is speaking all the time, we have other voices to contend with – the world, the flesh and the devil. The world speaks to our souls, the flesh to our bodies, and the devil to our minds. As believers, I don't believe the enemy has access to our spirits. That is holy ground.

But he is a deceiver, and (sadly) we are easily persuaded. Were it not so, Adam and Eve would have told the snake where to go, and we'd have no Bible and no cross. So if the thought comes into our <u>heads</u>, it may be the enemy. But if it bubbles up from our spirits, it is the Lord.

Secondly, if it is contrary to scripture, it's the enemy. Thirdly, if it is contrary to the Lord's character, it's not the Lord. What is its motivation? Is it *envy and selfish ambition* (see James 3:16)? Or is it *pure... peace-loving, considerate, submissive, full of mercy and good fruit, impartial and sincere* (James 3:17).

Let us not allow fear of the enemy's voice to hinder us from doing what the Lord has called us to. We are his sheep—we know the Lord's voice.

Tips for Getting Started

Prophecy is Spirit to spirit. It is speaking out of your spirit and into your mind, not the other way round. The mistake many make is wanting to understand what is rising up inside you before speaking it out. But remember, the Lord's thoughts are higher than our thoughts. We often won't understand it.

Go with your first impressions

In our sessions, we invite our delegates to take paper and pen, and ask the Lord for a word. Avoiding time to process, I usually only give them thirty seconds. Then they quickly write it or draw the picture. The Lord is faithful to answer when we ask, and it's almost always the first thought, word, or picture we receive that comes from him.

Once the word is on paper, we then invite them to ask the Lord who in the room the paper is for and give it to them. Many times we've seen some amazing confirmations. In one meeting, someone received exactly the same prophecy from three different people. That was encouraging!

Don't try to rationalise

When we try to process the impression, we often smother it. People say, "It didn't make sense." No, it may not. Remember, the messages are not for us, they are for others. In another meeting, a girl received two words: sunflower and sardines. And the Spirit even showed her the lady to share them with. Shaking, the girl obeyed.

When she heard the words, the recipient roared with laughter. "My name means sunflower, and to keep warm we've been sleeping in one bed like sardines!"

If you have just one word, begin

The Lord will give you the rest as you flow with the Holy Spirit.

Just say what you have and stop

If it's hard to start, it can be harder to stop. Once we are over the initial hurdle of embarrassment or fear, most of us feel we have to add more than the Lord is saying. We end up with too much John Fergusson and not enough of the Lord. But don't worry—we're learning. We didn't learn to ride a bicycle the first time either.

Prophecy in Church

Sadly, in most meetings prophecy is neglected. So many services follow the same pattern: worship, prayers, notices, offering, sermon, song, coffee. Why do we do it? Do we feel we've then "done God" for the week? Lord, forgive us. *In those days the word of the LORD was rare; there were not many visions* (1 Samuel 3:1).

But it's changing, by God's grace. This is what the Bible has in mind: *When you come together, <u>everyone</u> has a hymn, or a word of instruction, a revelation, a tongue or an interpretation. All of these must be done for the strengthening of the church.*

Two or three prophets should speak, and the others should weigh carefully what is said. And if a revelation comes to someone who is sitting down, the first speaker should stop. For <u>you can all prophesy</u> in turn so that everyone may be instructed and encouraged. The spirits of prophets are subject to the control of prophets. For God is not a God of disorder but of peace (1 Corinthians 14:26, 29-33).

Come with, not for

Today we can produce good music, good teaching and a great atmosphere. That's fine—excellence honours the Lord. But it risks falling into the entertainment trap by designing meetings around what people are coming for.

"Great message," people say as they leave. "I love that new song." "Shame about the coffee." And we adjust the services to accommodate people's expectations. We even improve the coffee. (There's nothing wrong with that!) But it's not church as the Lord planned it. It's spiritual entertainment.

"No one is to appear before me empty-handed," says the Lord, in Exodus 34:20, a concept repeated regularly in the Old Testament. The purpose is sacrifice. No longer animals, thank God, but shouldn't we still be dedicating our time, our talents, our finance, and developing our spiritual gifts *so that everyone may be instructed and encouraged*?

Our meetings are called services. They should be places where we serve each other. The question, "What do we go to church <u>for</u>?" should be reversed. What are we going with? What are we bringing to the meeting that will serve others and glorify the Lord? The Bible tells us: <u>*everyone*</u> *has a hymn, or a word of instruction, a revelation, a tongue or an interpretation.*

> What are we going to church with?

If this means what it says (and doesn't it?) it must include the elderly and the young, men and women, even new believers! *Two or three prophets should speak...* will it always be one hundred percent accurate? Of course not, which is why we are to test everything, *weighing carefully what is said*.

The picture here is a dynamic flow of the Holy Spirit in the meeting, with everyone actively participating. When unbelievers hear accurate prophecies they'll be truly convicted. When new believers see other new believers stepping out and trying to prophesy, and their words carefully considered, they'll be encouraged to have a go themselves. And when the Spirit has given someone revelation when reading their Bible during the week, and they share it, how great is their joy!

And if a revelation comes to someone who is sitting down, the first speaker should stop. In forty years as a believer, and thirty-five in ministry, I have never seen it happen. Perhaps we don't believe the folk in our congregations can have revelations themselves? Perhaps we are afraid of chaos? For it takes faith-filled, discerning leadership to manage such a meeting. But that too, is a gift of the Spirit.

However, there is still a piece of the Lord's plan missing.

Release the body

If you are not yet a leader, prayerfully ask your leaders to consider these things. And if they are not yet ready, return to prayer. For this <u>must</u> be the Lord's will for our meetings. He wrote the book.

If you are a pastor or leader, may I encourage you to teach prophecy, train your people and release them in your meetings? Is it a risk? Yes—all steps of faith are risky. But *God is not a God of disorder but of peace.* How then can we introduce prophecy safely?

Everything should be done in a fitting and orderly way (1 Corinthians 14:40). *Fitting* means it is culturally acceptable and fits with the way we do things. Every church has its own God-ordained culture, and how we include the gifts of the Spirit should match that. *Orderly* means we plan, but at the same time, allow the Spirit to flow as he wills. Have a plan, but be willing to change.

Twice in this passage of scripture, Paul speaks of those who don't understand. People will only come to understand if they are taught. After teaching this material at a pastors' conference in Nepal, one pastor said, "This teaching will completely change our meetings." Praise God! Teaching must come first.

Once our people understand, it's important to honour those who've taken the time to learn, practice and hone their gift. Some will be good, and need to be encouraged to step out and prophesy in our meetings. Once they have proved themselves, we can recognise their gift publicly, appointing them to the office of prophet or prophetess.

This is vital, for *the spirits of prophets are subject to the control of prophets* (1 Corinthians 14:32). In order to maintain the level of control the Lord wants in our meetings, we need prophets and prophetesses to discern what is of the Holy Spirit and what isn't. Without them in our churches, we risk disruption, division or false teaching creeping in—the very things we wish to avoid.

Prophets should have the gift of discernment to a higher degree. We shouldn't have to rely on our pastors and leaders, who may not have such a refined gift. Therefore the training and appointment of prophets and prophetesses enables the very control that we need to maintain the godly order we all seek.

Some churches give time during the service for the exercise of the gifts, when the congregation are invited to share what they have brought, whether prophecies or revelations.

In larger meetings, people can be encouraged to write out their prophecies, handing them to the leaders (if there are no prophets present) for approval. If it fits with the flow of the meeting, the leader can share it from the front.

If you have recognised prophets or prophetesses, they can be given authority to share whatever they believe is from the Lord at any appropriate moment. Trainees can share their words first of all with the prophets, and then, if suitable, from the platform.

Test Everything

Do not put out the Spirit's fire; do not treat prophecies with contempt. Test everything. Hold on to the good. Avoid every kind of evil (1 Thessalonians 5:19-22). Not everything will be from the Lord, but false prophets and false prophecy are quite different, and need to be handled differently.

False prophets

False prophets are sent by the enemy to disrupt, divide and destroy the church. Usually unaware of their true mission, they believe they've been sent by God to bring correction. We tell them by two main things.

Their message

In 2 Corinthians 11:4, Paul is rebuking that church for their willingness to accept false teaching. *For if someone comes to you and preaches a Jesus other than the Jesus we preached, or if you receive a different spirit from the one you received, or a different gospel from the one you accepted, you put up with it easily enough.*

He highlights the three red flags of a false message. Firstly, <u>a different Jesus</u>, meaning one who is either man or God, but not both; or one who is a great teacher, but not the Son of God; or one who is a prophet, but not the Messiah. No! Jesus is the Christ, the Son of God, who came in the flesh.

> We tell false prophets by their wrong message and their bad fruit

The second red flag is preaching a <u>different spirit</u>, referring to the Holy Spirit as a thing and not a Person; a power and not God; independent and not part of the Trinity. No! The Holy Spirit is just as much God as the Father and the Son, and one of the three Persons of the Trinity.

The third red flag is a <u>different gospel</u>, suggesting we can be saved through obeying the law, through circumcision, or through our own works. No! The true gospel declares we are saved by grace only through faith in the death of Jesus Christ on the cross to take away our sins, and in his resurrection.

Their fruit

In Matthew 7:15-20, Jesus warns that false prophets come in sheep's clothing, meaning outwardly they appear to be like us. So we can't tell them by their gifts, appearance or position. They can be funny, articulate, clever and persuasive! Jesus said, *"By their fruit you will recognise them."* There are three kinds of fruit:

Fruit of the Spirit (see Galatians 5:22-23) meaning *love, joy, peace, patience, kindness, goodness, faithfulness, gentleness and self-control.* Does the person demonstrate these qualities?

Fruit of the kingdom, meaning the things Jesus told his disciples to do in Matthew 10:8, as they preached the kingdom of God: *Heal the sick, raise the dead, cleanse those who have leprosy, drive out demons. Freely you have received, freely give.* Is the person healing, casting out demons, and seeing the lost saved? And doing it free of charge?

Fruit of their influence, meaning the reaction they have on others. Are they causing unity or division? Are they disturbing people's spirit or bringing peace? Are they honouring the leadership or speaking against it?

Some years ago, a man attended a retreat I was speaking at. He was gifted, artistic and helpful. But later we learned he'd been taking people aside in secret and "prophesying" over them. His words brought guilt, condemnation and fear. Some of his victims needed months of counselling.

As false prophets are usually arrogant (see 2 Peter 2 and Jude), we can ask a new person who wishes to speak to remain quiet at first. If they refuse, they have a rebellious spirit. If they humbly accept, they are more likely to be genuine.

But false prophets will always damage our churches and must be corrected, invited to repent, and if not, asked to leave. If again they refuse, the situation should be made public (see Matthew 18:15-20).

False prophecy

However, false prophecy happens all the time. Every prophet makes mistakes—in fact one way to tell they're real is they admit it. (I very much want this book to be of God, anointed by the Holy

Spirit. The truth is some will just be John Fergusson. I trust the Lord to show you which is which.)

It takes courageous and wise leadership to bring correction in public in a way that encourages the person, while correcting wrong thinking or theology. Again, it helps having prophets in the house who can bring discernment to doubtful words. So don't dismiss the genuine learners.

Therefore, my brothers, be eager to prophesy, and do not forbid speaking in tongues. But everything should be done in a fitting and orderly way (1 Corinthians 14:39-40).

Prophecy is essential for the church to grow and become all that the Lord wants it to be. In fact, without using the gifts of Spirit, given specifically *for the common good*, the church is a disabled bride. Let us choose to adopt the Lord's methods, and honour our Bridegroom. Let us surrender our meetings to the Holy Spirit.

We are building a picture of what that might look like. But we find further wisdom on flowing with the Spirit in a well-known passage in the Old Testament.

Chapter 10

How the Spirit Flows

Some years ago, while still very green, I was booked to address a gathering of very senior pastors and bishops. In holy fear, I sought the Lord. "How can I teach them?" And the Lord gave me revelation from this passage, a parable of revival, I have never heard anywhere else.

God's Mandate for Revival

Several times in this book I've suggested inviting and allowing the Holy Spirit to flow in our meetings. But how does that work? What does it look like in practice?

I love the Bible. As it's all there for a reason, I try to read everything. But I confess, plodding through Ezekiel 40 to 48 is tough.

These chapters describe the new temple. While it's easy to get bogged in the details of measurements, gates, and land division, it helps to remember it is a parable of the kingdom of God: ordered, precise, perfect, filled with beauty and the presence of the Prince of glory, although it may never be seen this side of the new earth.

But towards the end of these chapters, we have this jewel in Ezekiel 47:

> [1]*The man brought me back to the entrance of the temple, and I saw*

water coming out from under the threshold of the temple toward the east (for the temple faced east). The water was coming down from under the south side of the temple, south of the altar.

²He then brought me out through the north gate and led me around the outside to the outer gate facing east, and the water was flowing from the south side.

³As the man went eastward with a measuring line in his hand, he measured off a thousand cubits and then led me through water that was ankle-deep.

⁴He measured off another thousand cubits and led me through water that was knee-deep. He measured off another thousand and led me through water that was up to the waist.

⁵He measured off another thousand, but now it was a river that I could not cross, because the water had risen and was deep enough to swim in—a river that no one could cross.

⁶He asked me, "Son of man, do you see this?" Then he led me back to the bank of the river.

⁷When I arrived there, I saw a great number of trees on each side of the river.

⁸He said to me, "This water flows toward the eastern region and goes down into the Arabah, where it enters the Sea. When it empties into the Sea, the water there becomes fresh.

⁹Swarms of living creatures will live wherever the river flows. There will be large numbers of fish, because this water flows there and makes the salt water fresh; so where the river flows everything will live.

¹⁰Fishermen will stand along the shore; from En Gedi to En Eglaim there will be places for spreading nets. The fish will be of many kinds—like the fish of the Great Sea.

¹¹But the swamps and marshes will not become fresh; they will be left for salt.

¹²Fruit trees of all kinds will grow on both banks of the river. Their

leaves will not wither, nor will their fruit fail. Every month they will bear, because the water from the sanctuary flows to them. Their fruit will serve for food and their leaves for healing" (Ezekiel 47:1-12).

As I studied, I became intrigued by the great detail: directions, distances, trees, fish... Let's try to unwrap it.

The river flows from the temple located on *a very high mountain* (Zion) down to the Jordan valley (the Arabah) and into the Dead Sea, referred to in scripture as the Salt Sea, or the Sea of Arabah; Zechariah (14:8) calls it the "Eastern Sea" to distinguish from the "Western Sea" or Mediterranean. Since the Salt Sea is four hundred metres below sea level, the drop in height over a short distance is significant. This river isn't a trickle.

There are many symbols of the Holy Spirit—fire, wind, oil, water. Here it's a river—alive, refreshing, life-giving and powerful. In Zechariah, it appears on the occasion of the "day of the Lord", meaning the final battle against the devil. In his picture it divides, half flowing east and half, west. We find it again in the Holy City, the New Jerusalem, in Revelation 22:1, where it is *the river of the water of life*.

Is this only for the coming kingdom? I don't believe so. For although the kingdom of God is still to come, it is also here now, incomplete, but already begun. *"The kingdom of God is within you,"* Jesus says. Besides, the Spirit doesn't change; if this is the way he works in the coming kingdom, he will work the same way today.

So the river is a parable of the flow of the Holy Spirit. If this is so, we need to understand his ways. Let's see what happens.

The source

The water was *coming down from under the threshold of the temple*. The temple was located on the highest point. So the water wells up from a miraculous spring on the mountain-top under the temple. Only the Lord could do that.

The temple is the holy place, signifying the throne of the Lord. So the Spirit flows from God and never from anywhere or anyone else. As we have seen, there are no other holy spirits. The flow is pure, perfect, unadulterated by mankind; fresh every day, like the manna in the desert, like *rhema* words; moving, never stationary, welling up from the throne, running its own course down to where it is most needed.

Now *the temple faced east*, meaning the temple was orientated so the main doors faced east. The holy of holies was therefore on the west side. There were doors on the north and south sides, but none on the west. But the eastern doors were reserved for the Prince, so the man led Ezekiel out through the north doors or gate, and around to the outer gate in the east. The outer gate is the gate in the outer courtyard that led out of the temple complex and into the world.

But although the river was flowing eastwards, it wasn't coming from under the east side of the temple. It flowed *from under the south side*. Why? Well, what happens on the south side?

When Moses set up the tabernacle, *he placed the lampstand in the Tent of Meeting opposite the table on the south side of the tabernacle* (Exodus 40:24). All the items in the temple are symbolic, so what does the lampstand represent? Here is Revelation 1:20: *The mystery of the seven stars that you saw in my right hand and of the seven golden lampstands is this: The seven stars are the angels of the seven churches, and the seven lampstands are the seven churches.*

> The Holy Spirit flows to the world only through the church

So the river is flowing from under the lampstand, which represents the church. The Holy Spirit flows out to the world via the church. There is no other river, so he only flows through the church. What a privilege! But what a responsibility also. We are the guardians of the flow of the Holy Spirit to the world. Revival will only happen through the church.

The direction

The river flowed eastwards, towards the sunrise, towards a new day, towards new life. He flows away from the west and the Mediterranean Sea. In Israel, the sea meant trouble, often symbolising death. Jonah was three days in the sea, a sign of the Lord's death. In the new heaven and new earth in Revelation 21:1, *there was no longer any sea,* and two verses earlier we read that death and Hades had been thrown into the lake of fire. So the river flowed away from death towards life.

But because of the references to crossing the river, I had misread the next passage for years. Let's look carefully, as it's critical. *³As the man went <u>eastward</u> with a measuring line in his hand, he measured off a thousand cubits and then <u>led me</u> through water that was ankle-deep.*

Which way was the man leading Ezekiel? Eastwards. So? Which way was the river flowing? Eastwards. So the man was not leading Ezekiel across the river. <u>He was leading him downriver</u>. The image is clear.

We cannot walk across where the Spirit is going. We cannot cross the Holy Spirit. If we want revival, we must flow with the river. The anointing flows where the Spirit goes. What is the Holy Spirit doing in our church, our area, our town, our nation? Where in the world is he moving? We must go where he is flowing.

Now a thousand cubits is five hundred yards, or four hundred and fifty metres—no small distance. We must be willing to be led through unfamiliar waters for some time. Flowing with the Spirit is not a quick fix for our church. "We'll jump in the river, and revival will break out!" Sorry, we've got a long way to go yet. Revivals start small. They are built on persistent prayer, perseverance through difficulty, pressing on when nothing seems to change. The Lord's "suddenlies" rarely come suddenly.

In fact, for some it may not come at all. Hebrews 11:39 tells us the faithful were commended for their faith, *yet none of them received what had been promised*. Why not? Because they were laying foundations for generations to come. Salisbury cathedral took one hundred years to build. The men who dug its foundations never saw it, except with the eyes of vision.

But thank God for their faithfulness, because *God had planned something better for us so that only together with us would they be made perfect* (Hebrews 11:40). Astonishing. Their faithful perseverance is made complete in our participation in the fruit of their labours. They sow the seed; we reap the harvest, and thereby fulfil not only our own destiny, but theirs too. Then the sower and reaper will rejoice together.

We may well be called to similar efforts, seeing little. The explorer and missionary, David Livingstone, led one man to Christ, who backslid. A century later, in the same field where Livingstone was believed to have preached, Reinhard Bonnke saw tens of thousands saved. I don't doubt the great explorer rejoiced with the cloud of witnesses in heaven.

The tests

So we are being led downriver. As we follow, the river gets deeper—ankles, knees, waist, then out of our depth. Why? For the first three, we are being led. As we flow deeper with the Holy

Spirit, I believe these stages represent tests we need to overcome.

Ankles

The image of the prophet joyfully splashing in the ankle-deep water makes me smile. He was willing to be led into the river, willing to get his feet wet. He could have walked down the riverbank, watching the man splash, but he followed.

A shallow river isn't powerful. But it's different from the bank. Are we willing to move out of our comfort zones, putting away the familiar, and enter an alien environment? People won't like it. People will complain. People will wonder what on earth we're up to.

So the test of the ankle-deep water is obedience. Are we ready to follow? Will we stay in the river, allowing ourselves to be led, even though not much seems to be happening? Asking ourselves, "Where are the lost? Why has half my church left? I thought this was the river." The first thousand cubits test our obedience. Are we willing?

Knees

As we flow downstream, the river deepens and the challenges increase. Standing in a fast-flowing river up to our knees takes strength, perseverance and careful balance. The rocks shift under our feet. We wobble and correct.

Knees also represent prayer. Now we are being led to overcome difficulties, to persevere in prayer and hold on to the vision. We will need to be flexible—to "shift foot" when the riverbed moves. This stage of the journey can seem endless, applying all our strength as we

> As we flow with the river, it strengthens and grows

faithfully follow the flow.

But notice what is happening to the river. It is growing in power, depth and spread. As we flow with the river, it grows. Our very obedience and perseverance enables the river to become more powerful. As we flow with the Spirit he is able to do far more. So knees represent perseverance. How hungry are we?

Waist

Many revivals fail at this stage.

The clothing of the day didn't have pockets as we know them; they are not mentioned in scripture. Instead, money and valuables were hidden in folds of the garments, or tucked into their belts. So Ezekiel's river had now risen to the level of his money-belt.

Now "waist" can also be a coarse euphemism. When Rehoboam became king, the Israelites asked him to lift Solomon's heavy burden of taxation. His young friends advised him to refuse, saying, "My little finger is thicker than my father's waist." This was incredibly rude, as they didn't mean waist. Solomon had a thousand wives and concubines, but only three children. Rehoboam had twenty-eight sons and sixty daughters. So when we read "waist" in scripture, it may well mean "loins".

Together the two images represent integrity.

As revival begins to flow, people are attracted. The spotlight turns on us. Can we handle it? We will be tested in two main areas—money and sex. I don't need to provide examples as you will already know several. But I believe it is one reason why the Lord allows the long process of thousands of cubits of obedience and perseverance, which also hone our characters to be ready for the

> We will be tested in two main areas—money and sex

coming challenges. So the third stage tests our integrity. Are we truly dedicated?

But at the waist level, another thing happens. Standing up to our waist in a fast-moving river is almost impossible. The bottom becomes less secure. We are less dependent on our own weight and strength. We may even get carried along sometimes. And so comes the final stage.

Out of our depth

⁵He measured off another thousand, but now it was a river that I could not cross, because the water had risen and was deep enough to swim in—a river that no one could cross. As I said, because "cross" is mentioned twice, I thought Ezekiel was crossing the river. I was wrong. He is describing a river that is not too wide, but too <u>powerful</u> to cross. It is beyond anyone's ability.

So there is only one thing left to do: take our feet off the bottom and swim. Let the river take us. Our own strength, weight or abilities are now useless. And notice too that Ezekiel was no longer being led, as there was no need. Once we have surrendered to the Holy Spirit, we don't need anyone else leading. There's no risk of us going anywhere else. We just flow. So this final test is surrender.

Have we got our feet off the bottom? Have we given up relying on our best efforts, our best sermons, our best programmes, even our best people? Now the Spirit can do what he wants to do.

The Fruit

⁶He asked me, "Son of man, do you see this?" Then he led me back to the bank of the river. ⁷When I arrived there, I saw a great number of trees on each side of the river. We were having such a wonderful time in the river we had to be led back to the bank to see its full impact. Philip was having such a great time in Samaria, an angel had to appear to get him to go to the Ethiopian eunuch.

Life

Travelling east from Jerusalem you first pass through the Judean desert before descending the scarp of the Arabah to Jericho. As this river rushes through the desert, it brings life wherever it flows, a verdant ribbon in a sepia landscape.

Churches flowing with the Spirit are not only alive, they imbue life—new believers, people being baptised with the Holy Spirit with excitement and zeal. *Blessed are those whose strength is in you, who have set their hearts on pilgrimage. As they pass through the Valley of Baca [weeping], they make it a place of springs; the autumn rains also cover it with pools* (Psalm 84:5-6). These are believers determined to walk the second mile, to do whatever it takes, whatever it costs. Salt and light.

Miracles

Look at the river's effect on the Salt Sea. *⁸He said to me, "This water flows toward the eastern region and goes down into the Arabah, where it enters the Sea. When it empties into the Sea, the water there becomes fresh."*

The Dead Sea is thirty-five percent salt. Brine is a preservative, killing almost everything, hence the modern name. When fresh water enters salt water, it mixes, diluting the sea. For the Salt Sea to <u>become</u> fresh is a miracle.

The Jericho spring produced bad water, making the surrounding land unproductive. The citizens asked Elisha to help (2 Kings 2:19-22). He threw in a bowlful of salt, and the spring became fresh. Today it is named Elisha's spring. I have tasted it, and it's still just as good. Moses did the same thing with a piece of wood in the desert. Miracles are signs the river is flowing.

I have witnessed gold dust, oil flowing from someone's hand, jewels, holy clouds and seen photos of supernatural flames. "But, John," you may ask, "why on earth would the Holy Spirit do such things? Isn't this just the devil trying to deceive us with spurious signs?"

Well, the Spirit is God. He can do what he likes. Jesus didn't need to walk on water. He didn't need to feed five thousand people. He didn't need to be transfigured on the mountain. He didn't need to turn water into wine, although all were Messianic signs.

But let us ask ourselves, what is the fruit? Are people getting saved? Are they declaring, "Jesus is Lord!" Only the Spirit will do that (see 1 Corinthians 12:3).

Many years ago, an Indian pastor returned home from church one Sunday with his family. The dining table was bare. He and his wife took their children's hands. One child prayed, "Lord Jesus, we need some food and you said you provide for us." At that moment, a house crow landed on the table with a hundred rupee note in its beak. It dropped the money and flew away. In those days, that could buy several days' food.

The following Sunday, a distressed lady approached the pastor. "Please forgive me, pastor. Last Sunday the Lord told me to give you a hundred rupees. I took it from my purse, but it was such a large amount I changed my mind. As I went to put it back, a crow came down and snatched it away."

Fish

⁹Swarms of living creatures will live wherever the river flows. There will be large numbers of fish, because this water flows there and makes the salt water fresh; so where the river flows everything will live.

The <u>purpose</u> of revival is new believers. The <u>measure</u> of revival is new believers—large numbers of fish. Swarms suggests millions. I believe we are entering a time of an unprecedented move of God throughout the world. Nations formally totally closed to the gospel are seeing millions come to Christ.

For the <u>promise</u> of revival is also new believers! Nothing in the world is more important than people coming to Christ. Reinhard Bonnke said, "The church which is not saving the lost is lost itself." If we lose our focus for reaching the lost, we have lost our focus altogether. A church flowing in the Spirit wins souls.

> A church flowing in the Holy Spirit will harvest many fish

We read in the next verse that *the fish will be of many kinds—like the fish of the Great* [Mediterranean] *Sea.* The Lord loves variety; he is a creator, not a manufacturer. We are all unique, reflecting the nature of the Lord himself, and he meets us where we are. We've had the privilege of worshiping Jesus in cathedrals with liturgy and incense; on the top floor of wealthy banks; in humble homes of mud and thatch; in building sites in Indian slums; and in the open air with crowds a million strong.

Fishermen

[10]*Fishermen will stand along the shore; from En Gedi to En Eglaim there will be places for spreading nets.* Ezekiel's vision is radical! In the Spirit, he sees one of the most desolate places on earth coming alive with industry.

En Gedi and En Eglaim are villages on the shores of the Dead Sea. En Eglaim is only mentioned in the Bible here. Its location is unknown, but it must have been some distance from En Gedi, situated about half way down the western bank. So there were hundreds of fishermen.

Sharing the gospel is the privilege of every believer. In their radical book, *T4T – A Discipleship Re-Revolution,* Steve Smith and Ying Kai describe how, as soon as they lead someone to Christ, they teach them to share the gospel <u>immediately</u> with their friends and family. And as soon as the new believers win their friends, they pass on the same teaching. The resulting multiplication won 1.8 million people to Christ in ten years.

Revival isn't one man on a platform preaching the gospel, although that is also wonderful and productive. True revival is every believer so filled with the Spirit they cannot contain the gospel. In nations where the Spirit is flowing, people don't talk much about sport, or movies or their latest exploits. They talk about Jesus.

Fishermen don't need to be experts—they just need to be in the river. Jesus said, *"Whoever believes in me, as the Scripture has said, streams of living water will flow from within him." By this he meant the Spirit* (John 7:38-39a). The word "En" in Hebrew means "spring".

Healing

¹²Fruit trees of all kinds will grow on both banks of the river. Their leaves will not wither, nor will their fruit fail. Every month they will bear, because the water from the sanctuary flows to them. Their fruit will serve for food and their leaves for healing."

Fruit trees represent people. And wherever they go, if they are filled with the Spirit they <u>will</u> bear fruit. As leaders, we only need to release them. The Lord will do the rest.

Currently, the main focus of JF Ministries is teaching ordinary believers to heal the sick. Our schools are very practical. We merely invite people to apply a mustard seed of faith and do what

Jesus did—lay hands on sick people; command healing; ask the person to do something different; or simply pronounce the word of healing.

We don't read that Jesus prayed for the sick. He didn't even tell his disciples to pray for them. He just told them to heal. (See my books *Heal the Sick!* and *School of Healing Manual* for more.)

Jesus said, *"Heal the sick who are there, and tell them, 'The kingdom of God is near you'"* (Luke 10:9). When we do what he told us to do, he will do what he promised to do.

We have witnessed thousands healed under the hands of beginners. A seven-year old daughter laid hands on her mother suffering from carpel tunnel syndrome. She was instantly healed. A teenager, a few hours old in Christ, healed her own grandmother of arthritis. A line of twenty suffering from eye problems were all healed in a few minutes. A man paralysed from birth walked to the platform to tell his story. In a small meeting this week a lady's shoulder was healed, and another cancelled a heart operation.

We are privileged to live in days when the church is flowing in healing. If you are not yet seeing healing as part of the overflow of the Spirit in your life, step out in faith and begin. The Lord is faithful and he will do it. *Every month they will bear.* There is no season for revival. When the river flows, it's always revival.

We cannot control the Holy Spirit. We can only invite him and trust him with the consequences. They may not be what we expect, but if our hearts are willing, we will rejoice. Let him run our meetings!

However, there is one vital verse we left out of this chapter. Let's study verse 11, because it has a great deal to teach us about why revival may not be happening in our church or our lives.

Chapter 11

Why the Spirit Stops

We love rules.

When someone entrusted with a responsibility fails, we invent a rule "so that it doesn't happen again." When corporations or public bodies fail, we pass legislation that binds the rest of us in a web of bureaucracy. The irony is that this addresses the symptom, not the problem, which is the human heart. So before long the someone or the organisation or the body finds a loophole. And we get more rules.

Bad behaviour leads to problems, which lead to regulations which lead to traditions, which lead (in our churches) to religion—obeying the rules without a change of heart.

Why do we do it, and what has this to do with revival? The motive for most of this rule-making is fear. Fear of further failures; of people getting hurt; of misunderstandings and divisions. Fear of losing our position, our fruit, our people, and our place.

This of course was the mindset of the Pharisees toward Jesus, who in their eyes broke the rules in spades. *"What are we accomplishing?"* they asked. *"Here is this man performing many miraculous signs. If we let him go on like this, everyone will believe in him, and then the Romans will come and take away both our place and our nation"* (John 11:47b-8). People won't understand. People will leave. The government/leadership/council will close us down. Fear.

And it seeps into revivals too. Ezekiel 47:11 is a parable of interrupted flow. Let's see what it can teach us.

Swamps and Marshes

In our story of revival, all had gone swimmingly until this: *But the swamps and marshes will not become fresh; they will be left for salt.* Here was no life, no fruit, no new believers, no healing. Just salt. What had happened?

Let me take you to a high mountain. It is raining. The water trickles, wherever gravity leads it, to join other rivulets into a tiny fold of the hillside. Before long, it becomes a bubbling creek, frothing over stones, eddying in small pools, tumbling out of control down the steep slopes. Here it is fresh, clean, full of life and sparkle, but without much power. Immature.

Soon, however, it drops into a broader valley and joins other streams, and becomes a significant river. It is fast, broad and powerful, too dynamic for anyone to cross. Over millennia, this river has carved out the valley it runs through, forcing obstacles or boulders aside. If dammed, it simply rises until it overflows, stripping the valley floor clean again. It changes the landscape.

And then it arrives at the plain. Now it widens and slows, meandering left to right and back again, picking up the sludge of the cities, then releasing the silt to form islands, and which in turn grow weeds and useless vegetation. The river no longer washes them away but separates into channels, seeking a way around the obstacles. Or it stops and stagnates. The vegetation rots and stinks. It has become a swamp. A marsh.

What has happened to our bubbling creek or valley-carving river? It has left its fall behind in the hills. Gravity, like Ichabod in 1 Samuel 4:21, has departed.

Perhaps we shouldn't be surprised that Jesus himself warns us about these very problems in the letters to the seven churches in the book of Revelation.

Implications for the Church

Above all, the church is the Lord's agent for change. We aren't a cosy club separated (or worse, hiding) from the world, but a stone in the world's boot, acting as the catalyst for people to turn to Christ.

A main theme of this book is that all this is impossible without the power of the Holy Spirit. We must get our feet off the bottom and overflow to the world outside. If not, swamps and marshes await.

Slow water

The moment the river leaves the hill, it slows. We become comfortable, familiar with our surroundings, with our friends, with our routines and services. Once we become self-sufficient—we have good music, good preachers and good programmes—we can do this church thing without needing the Spirit.

Worse, we've made things the way we like them, attracting those like us who like them too. So we resist change, and are uncomfortable around those different from us. Of course, we smile at them when they come, but later roll our eyes with our friends.

> The Lord is not the God of all comfortable

However, the Lord is the *God of all comforts*, not the God of all comfortable! If we were needing comfort, we must have been uncomfortable. Jesus says to the church in Sardis, *"I know your deeds; you have a reputation of being alive, but you are dead. Wake up! Strengthen what remains and is about to die, for I have not found your deeds complete in the sight of my God"* (Revelation 3:1-2).

Brian Houston, leader of Hillsong, Sydney, makes changes intentionally. Since we need to change ourselves, he believes we better get used to it. Change kills the twin demons of comfort and complacency.

Brian once said to my brother who works for him, "Robert, I'd like you to move your office." Robert had been located in the city campus for ten years, but the headquarters was on the other side of town.

"Of course," my brother said. "When would you like me to move?"

"Now!"

Two hours later, Robert and his team were settling into the Hills campus.

The seven churches in Revelation 2 and 3 faced difficulties that threatened their survival. Jesus rebukes five, while he encourages the two weak ones, Smyrna and Philadelphia, to persevere in their trials. And these difficulties reflect the problems of the river—the churches had lost their gravity.

At the beginning of each letter Jesus reveals an aspect of his nature. It came as a surprise to me to discover the solution hidden there for each of the church's problems. For it differs for each church.

For Sardis, he begins, *"These are the words of him who holds the seven spirits* [or sevenfold Spirit] *of God and the seven stars"* (Revelation 3:1). The stars are the angels (see Revelation 1:20), so Jesus means the solution to their laziness is to get back into the supernatural. They needed the Holy Spirit to wake them up. The Holy Spirit *is* revival, and we cannot expect supernatural results without him.

Meandering

Once our river has slowed, it begins to wander in long sweeping turns, first in one direction, then another, slowly seeking its torturous way to the sea. The twists become so exaggerated that at the next flood the sinuous river erodes its own banks, carving off oxbow lakes, stagnant pools of forgotten vision.

And once we lose our sense of direction, the purpose for which the Lord created us, we're immediately susceptible to the latest trends, peering over our shoulders to see what's working in that growing church over there.

> What is the prophetic foundation of your church?

Rodney Francis of New Zealand, a prophet and founder of Gospel Faith Messenger, says that every church has a prophetic foundation—the vision the Lord gave to the person or people who began the work, and which carries the Lord's long-term agenda for its success. Too often, new leadership fails to appreciate its importance and leads the church in another direction altogether.

And once we're willing to change direction, we are liable to be influenced by political pressure and theological compromise, adjusting the culture to suit the people. Fear of man. But *"If I were still trying to please men,"* Paul writes, *"I would not be a servant of Christ"* (Galatians 1:10). Political correctness is an enemy of the kingdom of God.

Jesus warns the church in Pergamum of the same thing. Unlike some others, they hadn't renounced their faith but remained true to his name. However, compromise had crept in through the back door: Balaamites and Nicolaitans.

The Old Testament prophet Balaam used his God-given gifts to get rich. When Balak, the Moabite king, brought Balaam to curse Israel, he could only bless them. Perhaps Balaam suggested sending pretty maidens into the Israelite camp. The result? Fornication and idolatry.

But who were the Nicolaitans? In Acts 15:29, the apostles instructed the growing church *to abstain from food sacrificed to idols, from blood, from the meat of strangled animals and from sexual immorality* (Acts 15:29). However, this meant Christians couldn't attend the festivals, earning them public disapproval. The Nicolaitans wanted to be free to eat anything. This meant they could join public festivals, which almost always ended in immorality. Fornication and idolatry again.

As before, we find the answer at the beginning of the passage: *"These are the words of him who has the sharp, double-edged sword"* (Revelation 2:12), meaning the word of God. Faith in the scriptures is always the solution to compromise. The warnings in Acts 15:29 all related to idol worship—we do well to avoid these things.

Although they hadn't denied the Name of Jesus, the church in Pergamum had lost its way, wandering from the truth, despite the clear instructions of the apostles. Revivals are founded on truth. The vision is to see the lost won, and the basis is the Bible. Nothing else works.

Divided stream

Covering almost 150,000 square kilometres, the Pantanal in South America is the world's largest tropical bog. Here the mighty Paraguay river slows and divides. Some years ago we had the privilege of spending several days there, winding through the narrow channels avoiding the caiman crocodiles and the hungry piranha.

In the mountains, the gurgling stream didn't notice obstacles. In the valley, the river, set firmly on its course, rose above them or washed them away. But now the islands of sludge spawn divisions. Shall we go this way? Or that?

"Well, you may go that way, but I will go this."

"I don't care. I won't have anything to do with *your* theology!"

While it was still the Soviet Union, I joined a mission's team to the Ukraine. Here we discovered that a whole denomination had split over whether to include foot washing in the meetings. There were the foot-washers and (presumably not so clean) non-foot-washers. However, the foot-washers then argued over whether foot washing should happen before or after Holy Communion. They split again. This would be hilarious if it wasn't true.

Division has been the bane of revival throughout the centuries. Here is Psalm 133:

How good and pleasant it is when brothers live together in unity!

It is like precious oil poured on the head, running down on the beard, running down on Aaron's beard, down upon the collar of his robes.

> Unity is an attitude

It is as if the dew of Hermon were falling on Mount Zion. For there the LORD bestows [The Hebrew is *siwwah*, meaning "commands"] *his blessing, even life forevermore.*

Life forevermore means salvation, and salvations are the gauge of revival. The overflowing oil is a symbol for the anointing, or the Holy Spirit. The dew of Hermon means consistent, regular, predictable moisture. Combined, these are powerful images; unity among the believers brings predictable, consistent anointing, where the Spirit flows without hindrance—revival!

Now unity is an attitude, choosing to be part of what the Lord is doing above our own preferences. I would rather be where God is blessing—more than that—where he *commands* a blessing, whether I like the theology or not; whether I like the music or not;

whether I like the preaching or not; even whether I like the people or not! My comfort zone is unimportant.

I attend a church (this is confession time) where the music is so loud I wear ear-plugs. But every week dozens are getting saved. There's a church down the road where I love the music. But few are coming to Christ there.

> The body cannot function with its arms and legs missing

Unlike the other five, the Lord didn't rebuke the churches in Smyrna and Philadelphia. Rather, he encouraged them because they were weak. Division weakens churches, separating the parts of the body into 'eye' (prophetic) churches, 'foot' (mission) churches or 'hand' (servant) churches. But where does the foot go, unless it has eyes? And how can the hand help, unless it has feet? *The eye cannot say to the hand, "I don't need you!" And the head cannot say to the feet, "I don't need you!"* (1 Corinthians 12:21). The Lord intends the body to work together.

There are millions of Christians around the world who don't attend a church. Often they have been hurt, or cannot find a church that suits them. This is tragic. For unity brings revival, and others need their gifts. The body cannot function with its arms and legs scattered to the four winds. If that's you, get over your hurts and preferences, get into a church and start serving. It doesn't matter if you like it or not. Who knows, you may be the key to their revival.

Silt

In the valley, the river carries the mud with it, washing away the problems, even rolling the stones across the bottom. But as the water slows, the fine silt forms sandbars, which become islands. This has further consequences, but firstly it hinders the flow.

Jesus commended the church in Ephesus for their

perseverance, hard work and righteousness. They hated the Nicolaitans, as did he. But they had forgotten that his kingdom is about relationship. They'd lost the joy of the mountain stream; they'd left behind the power of the landscaping river; they'd *forsaken their first love* (Rvelation 2:4).

Here is a situation we've seen before—depending on their own strength, burdening the church with tradition, bureaucracy, overwork and financial constraints. Sounds familiar? Silt. And it snarls the flow of the Spirit.

And the solution? There at the beginning again: *These are the words of him who holds the seven stars in his right hand and walks among the seven golden lampstands* (Revelation 2:1), means Jesus is with them. Just as the Lord walked in the Garden of Eden in the cool of the day, he longs for intimate fellowship. They don't need to do this thing on their own. Church is family, not business.

Only this morning the Lord reminded me too. "Relax, John, and enjoy the journey." As someone who likes to keep active, I need to hear it regularly. It's not about what we can do, but what he can do. Revival is him, not us.

Useless vegetation

It's remarkable that despite the abundance of water and fertility, we rarely farm these marshes. They may produce reeds for thatching, or papyrus for scrolls. But no crops grow there; no forest or fruit trees; no vines or fig trees. Saline marshes seem to fare even worse, harbouring a few salt-tolerant grasses, or in the tropics, mangroves, not even useful as firewood.

The church in Thyatira had fallen further from grace than Pergamum. The Lord praised them for their deeds, their love and faith, their service and perseverance. They were even doing more than they did at first, but the church had become dominated by the teaching of Jezebel.

The wife of Ahab king of Israel, Jezebel centralised Baal worship in that country, and manipulated Ahab into becoming her puppet. The church in Pergamum had just gone a little off-track, the Lord reminding them of his word. But Jezebel was teaching Thyatria *satan's so-called deep secrets* (Revelation 2:24), leading them once more into immorality and idolatry. (Has the devil any new tricks?)

Where false teaching dominates, there will be no fruit. Here the Lord's solution is uncompromising—*"These are the words of the Son of God, whose eyes are like blazing fire and whose feet are like burnished bronze"* (Revelation 2:18). He is holy, and not to be messed with. He goes on (verse 23), *I will strike her children dead."* Wow. But there were some who didn't hold to her teaching, and the Lord encouraged them to hold on to what they have.

I have written elsewhere (see my book *Authority*) of the dangers of Jezebel in our churches. If present, he or she (the Jezebel spirit is not restricted to women) must be given time to repent, and if not, evicted. But there is one further consequence of restricted flow.

Stagnation

In many bogs, marsh gas bubbles to the surface, a mixture of methane and other gases, produced by anaerobic fermentation of rotting vegetation. Under certain conditions, this gas can ignite, causing an "atmospheric ghost-light" at night, often referred to as will-o'-the-wisp.

The church in Laodicea had fallen into the worst trap of all—pride. *"You say, 'I am rich; I have acquired wealth and do not need a thing'"* (Revelation 3:17). Not only had they forgotten their need of the Holy Spirit, they thought they could manage very well without him. Unlike the others, the Lord found no praise for them. After all, pride was at the root of the devil's temptation of Adam and Eve in the Garden, wanting to be like God.

All evil begins with pride. "I know better than God. I know better than his word or his plan or his purpose."

Pride blinds us to the truth, for Revelation 3:17 continues, *"You do not realize that you are wretched, pitiful, poor, blind and naked."*

"No, no! We have our own thing going. We even have our own fire."

At the ordination of Aaron and his sons, after they had fulfilled all the Lord's instructions and placed the sacrifices on the altar, *fire came out from the presence of the LORD and consumed the burnt offering and the fat portions on the altar. And when all the people saw it, they shouted for joy and fell facedown* (Leviticus 9:24). By this, the Lord approved their obedience, revealed his glory and participated in the ceremony!

However, Aaron's sons, Nadab and Abihu, had their own fire too, man-made fire, unauthorised fire, and they offered that before the Lord as well. Then real fire, the Holy Spirit, *came out from the presence of the Lord and consumed them* (Leviticus 9:2).

Thank the Lord he didn't destroy the Laodiceans, but urged them to repent. Praise God for his grace and patience with us too. But we need to heed his discipline: *"I counsel you to buy from me gold refined in the fire* [faith], *so you can become rich; and white clothes to wear* [righteousness], *so you can cover your shameful nakedness; and salve to put on your eyes* [humility], *so you can see"* (Revelation 3:18).

Let us welcome back gravity, the force that moves mountains. Let us avoid the dangers of slow water, division and silt. The Holy Spirit is revival—where he moves, revival happens. It's not something we can do, orchestrate or engineer ourselves. Let us continue to pray for his presence, and trust him with the results.

But the Spirit is also the Spirit of wisdom, so he can and does guide us to the place of revival. How?

Chapter 12

Making Godly Decisions

It seemed good to the Holy Spirit and us

As a child, I was afraid of mazes. For me, the embarrassment of getting lost outweighed the reward of finding the centre. At each turn, one way would be right, and one wrong. Which way? I would stand, chewing my fingernails.

Many feel the same when following the Lord. Which direction does the Lord want me to take? And we freeze in fear of making a wrong choice. But the kingdom of God isn't a maze—it's a family.

I have always said the Christian life is simple (though not easy). Listen to the Spirit and do what he says. Which is fine when he speaks, but what if he doesn't? When my wife and I needed guidance over our future and the Lord remained silent, I became frustrated. "I've got your name and address," he said, but still gave us no direction.

We were left to make our own decisions. And that's the point.

Listening to the Holy Spirit

I had been wrestling recently over whether to seek a traditional publisher for my latest book, or self-publish. Watching a worship video a few weeks ago at our weekly home group, an advert crawled across the bottom of the screen, "It's time to self-publish." Others saw it too, knowing that was for me. We replayed the video many times, and it wasn't there. The Spirit is so creative!

Jesus was led by the Spirit into the desert. Simeon was moved by the Spirit to go into the temple courts. When Paul returned to what is Turkey today to see how the churches he planted were doing, the Spirit of the Lord kept them from preaching in Asia and Bithynia (see Acts 16:6-7). We are not told how, but it could have been circumstances or just an uneasy feeling.

A few verses later we read, *during the night Paul had a vision of a man of Macedonia standing and begging him, "Come over to Macedonia and help us." After Paul had seen the vision, we got ready at once to leave for Macedonia, concluding that God had called us to preach the gospel to them* (Acts 16:9-10). Direction doesn't come much clearer than that.

After we had sold our farm, but still awaiting the Lord's plan for our lives, I was in worship one day, when the Lord gave me a vision.

I saw a pretty English church on a hill. Folk were emerging after a service, chatting and cheerful. To the right of the church, it was a sunny spring day, the elder bushes scenting the air. But to the left, all was grey and red. And in the black sky, stood a huge cross. It seemed the Lord was giving us a choice.

"I must go the way of the cross," I said. But it looked hard, so I asked the Lord what it meant. He lifted me, and we zoomed into the vision. Beyond the stark canyons and treeless landscape was a dot of light. As we neared, I could see what looked like a forest. Closer still, the white light became a platform and the forest, a huge crowd. Surrounding the people were real trees, but not English.

"But Lord, you said you'd bless us whichever choice we made." There on the right side, poised in the perfect blue sky, a tiny, silver cross. I knew then that the Lord was calling us to international evangelism. And two weeks later we received a call from Christ for all Nations to join the team.

It's exhilarating when we receive guidance like that. But I've only had one such vision in forty years as a Christian. The Lord spoke only three times in an audible voice to Jesus. It's not his usual way.

Growing up

When I was a child, I talked like a child, I thought like a child, I reasoned like a child. When I became a man, I put childish ways behind me (1 Corinthians 13:11). When we're a baby, our parents do everything for us: feeding us, dressing us, tying our shoes. A little older, we learn to dress ourselves; then to choose our own clothes; and finally to buy those we enjoy, probably to our parents' horror!

Maturing is the process of learning to make decisions. It is no different in the kingdom of God. Once we were babes in Christ. But we become sons. Galatians 4:1-7 explains:

What I am saying is that as long as the heir is a child [nepios], he is no different from a slave, although he owns the whole estate. He is subject to guardians and trustees until the time set by his father. So also, when we were children [nepioi], we were in slavery under the basic principles of the world. But when the time had fully come, God sent his Son [Huion], born of a woman, born under law, to redeem those under law, that we might receive the full rights of sons [huiothesian]. Because you are sons [huioi], God sent the Spirit of his Son [Huiou] into our hearts, the Spirit who calls out, "Abba, Father." So you are no longer a slave, but a son [huios]; and since you are a son [huios], God has made you also an heir.

In this passage we find two Greek words for children—*nepios*, which means an infant, literally, "one who cannot speak". The second word is *huios*, which means a mature son, old enough to inherit the father's estate.

Notice the small child is subject to guardians and trustees *until the time set by his father*. It was the father who decided when the child was sufficiently mature to be inducted into adulthood. Traditionally, this was at the bar mitzvah, around the age of twelve or thirteen, as we read in the story of Jesus in Luke 2:41-52. But the principle is greater than the tradition.

I believe fathers should be the ones releasing their children to be treated as adults, when he deems them mature enough. One of the greatest challenges as parents is releasing our children to make their own way as they mature. Equally, it is the Lord who deems us mature sons and releases us, once we have become his adopted children.

Is his heart in his mouth too? How did the father of the prodigal son in Luke 15 feel, when he gave him his inheritance? Surely he knew what his son was likely to do. But he was "of age", a *huios*, not a *nepios*, and able to make his own decisions, even if initially they proved disastrous. Later, of course, he *came to his senses* and returned to his father, who not only forgave him, but fully reinstated him.

Our decisions are right

As we mature in Christ, we become a *huios*, like him. Jesus said, *"But if I do judge, my decisions are right, because I am not alone. I stand with the Father, who sent me"* (John 8:16). In the same way, when we stand with the Father, our decisions will also be right. If we are walking with the Lord, filled with his Spirit, we can have confidence that our will is his will.

Therefore, like the Prodigal son, the Lord leaves us to make our own decisions, trusting them to be right. Some people feel they have to check in with the Lord over every little thing. No, no, we are no longer infants. The Lord expects us to be able to make good choices and act on them. In fact, he trusts us far more than we trust him, *because those who are led by the Spirit of God are sons* [huioi] *of God* (Romans 8:14).

And if we're wrong? There is even a Rescuer!

"This is what the LORD says—your Redeemer, who formed you in the womb: I am the LORD, who *has made all things, who alone stretched out the heavens, who spread out the earth by myself, who foils the signs of false prophets and makes fools of diviners, who overthrows the learning of the wise and turns it into nonsense, who carries out the words of his servants and fulfils the predictions of his messengers"* (Isaiah 44:24-26).

As we have seen, when false prophets make a prediction, the Lord works to ensure it doesn't happen. Equally, when his own servants do so, he works to fulfil their words. Despite our bad decisions or inaccurate prophecies, the Lord can work all things out for good. What grace! But also what freedom for us.

With this in mind, Paul writes in 2 Thessalonians 1:11-12, *we constantly pray for you, that our God may count you worthy of his calling, and that by his power <u>he may fulfil every good purpose of yours</u> and every act prompted by <u>your</u> faith. We pray this so that the name of our Lord Jesus may be glorified in you, and you in him, according to the grace of our God and the Lord Jesus Christ.*

Again, we see the Lord works to fulfil our own (good) purposes, and our own (faithful) actions. Why? So that the name of Jesus is glorified in us. He gives us the freedom to make our own decisions, trusting they will be good and faithful, and works to ensure an outcome that glorifies Jesus, however feeble our decision-making. What astonishing freedom!

We are his children, and godly parents always want them to grow up, which means letting them make their own decisions.

Is this risky? Of course. Faith takes risks. As his children then, we have this responsibility to make good choices. We cannot be frozen in indecision as I was in mazes. If the Lord trusts us to make good choices, we must step out and make them. As long as our heart is to please the Lord, it's better to do something wrong, than do nothing at all. As they say, you cannot move a parked car. At least if we are moving we can turn around.

Fortunately, when the Spirit doesn't seem to be speaking (or we're not hearing), he has surrounded us with other good advisors. But there is no room for arrogance. Humility respects and draws wisdom from his word, the counsel of friends, good teaching and preaching, the guidance of leaders—and his peace.

The judge of peace

When Paul returned to Troas, he found the Lord had opened a door for him to preach the gospel there. On his first visit, he'd had no opportunity being guided to Macedonia instead. Normally, he would have been delighted, thinking that the Lord had purposely led him back to Troas.

However, he writes in 2 Corinthians 2:13: *I still had no peace of mind, because I did not find my brother Titus there. So I said good-bye to them and went on to Macedonia.* Paul had an open door to preach the gospel in a place he must have wanted to, but his peace of mind was a greater guide of the Spirit's will.

When our spirit is troubled, it's important to pray it through until we come to a place of peace. It is likely the Spirit is guiding us to avoid whatever, or whoever, is troubling us.

> The Lord trusts you to make good decisions, so step out and make them

Let the peace of Christ rule [the Greek is brabeueto] *in your hearts, since as members of one body you were called to peace. And be thankful* (Colossians 3:15).

Brabeuo means to arbitrate, in other words, let the peace in your heart be the judge of whether something is of God or not. How can we be sure? Isn't that pretty subjective? True. But remember the Spirit of God lives in your spirit, and the Father himself is working everything out for good. The peace that passes understanding is more than a feeling—it's a vital signpost of the Lord's direction.

Urim and Thummim

In the Old Testament, the clothing of Aaron the high priest included an ephod on which was tied a *breastpiece for making decisions* (Exodus 28:15). Besides the twelve jewels representing the tribes of Israel, the breastpiece also housed the Urim and Thummim.

"Whenever Aaron enters the Holy Place, he will bear the names of the sons of Israel <u>over his heart</u> on the breastpiece of decision as a continuing memorial before the LORD. Also put the Urim and the Thummim in the breastpiece, so they may be <u>over Aaron's heart</u> whenever he enters the presence of the LORD. Thus Aaron will always bear the means of making decisions for the Israelites <u>over his heart</u> before the LORD" (Exodus 28:29-30).

When King David wanted to consult the Lord he called the high priest to bring the ephod. The king asked the Lord what he should do. And the high priest drew out one or other stone from the breastpiece. I understand one meant, "Yes", and the other, "No".

But the Exodus scripture says three times (and when the Bible says something three times in a passage, God is making a point), that the means of making decisions was *over his heart*. Peace in our hearts is a key to the Lord's guidance.

Many years ago we moved to Surabaya, Indonesia, to prepare a campaign for Reinhard Bonnke. One of our first tasks was to find somewhere to live. We hunted everywhere. After several weeks, we found a small house on the edge of town. It wasn't very clean, had no hot water, and was very... Indonesian. But we were tired of looking and agreed to take it.

That same day, a local businessman called us to follow him. He led us through the smart suburbs to some closed gates, which a servant opened. We drove into a large court and parked. The house was huge, with hot water, a western kitchen and staff. "The owner is moving to Jakarta," said the businessman. "You can have this free for as long as you stay." We were overwhelmed.

But that night my troubled spirit disturbed my sleep. When I finally slept, I dreamed of the big house, but it was full of bats. Clearly, the Lord wanted us to keep our word and take the small house. We reluctantly declined the businessman's generous offer. He was greatly offended.

It turned out that the small house was owned by a widow and had been empty for months. The rent was her only income. And I then remembered Luke 20:46-47: *"Beware of the teachers of the law…. They devour widows' houses and for a show make lengthy prayers. Such men will be punished most severely."* Thank you, Lord, for preventing a bad mistake. We rented the small house and were very happy there.

Let the peace of God rule in our hearts. That peace is the surest guide we have to the will of the Father. For this reason, we shouldn't make important decisions when we are tired, angry, frustrated, worried or fearful. These peace-robbers will steal our Urim and Thummim, the guidance of the Holy Spirit.

The mind of Christ

As we've seen, the Lord makes the astonishing claim that as believers we have the mind of Christ. *The spiritual man makes judgements about all things* (1 Corinthians 2:15). Romans 8:16 refers to this prompting as the Spirit testifying, or witnessing, with our spirit, the two in agreement.

Writing to the new believers the Council in Jerusalem wrote, *"It seemed good to the Holy Spirit and to us not to burden you with anything beyond the following requirements"* (Acts 15:28). With the mind of Christ, we too can say, "It seems good to the Spirit and to us."

As believers we have this amazing privilege—the peace of God in our hearts as a witness to his will and purpose. And when we make a decision, we can be confident our heavenly Father will work things out to bring glory to his Son through our choices.

What amazing grace and what astonishing freedom!

~ ✝ ~

From the beginning, the Father works all things through his Son, by the power of the Holy Spirit. Nothing happens without him. We have been made righteous in order to receive him. The baptism with the Holy Spirit is the Lord's weapon of choice for the growth of his kingdom and of the church.

It is ignorant folly to suggest we can build the church without the Lord's provision. Jesus said, *"I will build my church,"* and he will do it by the power of his Spirit, working through his people. He has no other agenda and no plan B.

I pray this book will have stirred your own spirit to be more hungry for the Word of God and to flow with the Holy Spirit in your life and meetings. I pray it inspires you to flow in the gifts of the Spirit to change the lives of those around you, leading many to Christ. That is why we are here.

May I leave you with this exhortation from James: *Do not merely listen to the word, and so deceive yourselves. Do what it says. But the man who looks intently into the perfect law that gives freedom, and continues to do this, not forgetting what he has heard, but doing it—he will be blessed in what he does* (James 1:22, 25).

Be blessed. Be active. And go on being filled with the Holy Spirit.

~ ✝ ~

If you have enjoyed this book, please review it on Amazon. John Fergusson can be contacted at johnf@jfm.org.nz.

Recommended Reading

Jack Deere, *The Beginner's Guide to the Gift of Prophecy*, (2001) Regal Books

John Bevere, *The Holy Spirit: an Introduction*, (2013) Messenger International

John Fergusson, *Authority*, JF Ministries

John Fergusson, *Heal the Sick!* JF Ministries

John Fergusson, *Holy Fire*, JF Ministries

John Fergusson, *School of Healing Manual*, JF Ministries

Reinhard Bonnke, *Holy Spirit: Revelation and Revolution*, E-R Productions

Reinhard Bonnke, *Mighty Manifestations*, (1994), Kingsway

Rodney Francis, *Developing Prophetic Ministry*, Gospel Faith Messenger

Steve Smith with Ying Kai, *T4T: A Discipleship Re-Revolution*, (2011), Wigtake Resources

Books available from JF Ministries

School of Healing Manual
A 52-page booklet available in many languages. Thousands have been healed using the simple Biblical principle that we should do what Jesus did, and not what he didn't do! Over 80,000 printed.

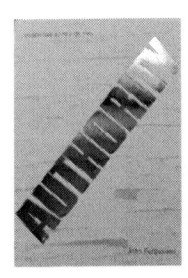

Authority
An in depth study that will revolutionise your understanding of the authority you have and how it works.

Reinhard Bonnke: "It is a must-read for all those who want more from God."

Who's in Charge Around Here?
Struggling with authority? A shorter version of *Authority* in easier English, more for believers than leaders.

Discover the amazing authority you have, and how it should work at home, at work and at church.

Holy Fire
Throughout scripture, the fire of God destroys the unholy and glorifies the holy. Kingsway UK said it's one of the more important books they published. This astonishing revelation explains why hell is an inevitable outcome of God's love.

Many more on www.jfm.org.nz.

About the author

John Fergusson came to Christ reading the Bible, hence his love of scripture. He was baptised with the Holy Spirit in Soweto in 1984 in Reinhard Bonnke's big tent.

He founded JF Ministries in 1998 to preach the gospel and spread the good news of the kingdom of God, especially in less reached parts of the world. The current focus of the ministry is Nepal, where the church is experiencing explosive growth.

He has trained tens of thousands to heal the sick, and seen many wonderful miracles under the hands of ordinary believers.

A former campaign director for Reinhard Bonnke, John has taught in Bible colleges, preached around the world, and is author of many books and booklets.

He was born in England, where he farmed for nearly twenty years. He now lives in Auckland, New Zealand, with his Kiwi wife, Bron.

Manufactured by Amazon.com.au
Sydney, New South Wales, Australia